THE SPINNER'S BOOK OF FLEECE

THE SPINNER'S BOOK OF FLEECE

A Breed-by-Breed Guide to Choosing and Spinning the Perfect Fiber for Every Purpose

Beth Smith

Foreword by Deborah Robson

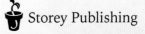
Storey Publishing

*The mission of Storey Publishing is to serve our customers by
publishing practical information that encourages
personal independence in harmony with the environment.*

Edited by Gwen Steege
Art direction and book design by Alethea Morrison
Text production by Liseann Karandisecky
Indexed by Nancy D. Wood

Cover and interior photography by John Polak, except for:
© Animals Animals/Superstock, 197 and 228;
© blickwinkel/Alamy, 34 (bottom); © Charles Stirling/
Alamy, 34 (top); © David Porter/Alamy, 136–137; © David
Ridley/Alamy, 221; © Elizabeth Ferraro, Apple Rose
Farm, 216–217; © F1 online digitale Bildagentur GmBH/
Alamy, 170; © FLPA/Alamy, 142–143; © Guy Edwardes/
naturepl.com, 178 (top); © Holger Burmeister/Alamy,
166–167; © Jason Smalley/naturepl.com, 124–125; © Jean
G. Green, 94–95; © Johncarnemolla/Dreamstime.com,
76–77; © John Van Decker/Alamy, 224–225; © Jouan Rius/
naturepl.com, 205; © Juniors Bildarchiv GmBH/Alamy,
208–209; © Kerry Hill/Dreamstime.com, 30; © Krystyna
Szulecka/Alamy, back cover (top) and 67; © Lynn Stone,
86–87; Mars Vilaubi, 172; © National Geographic Image
Collection/Alamy, 101; © Robert Canis/Alamy, 130–131;
© Sally Anne Thompson/animal-photography.com, 109;
© Stephen Dalton/Minden Pictures, 33; © Stephen
Taylor/animal-photography.com, 173; © Susan Gibson/
Alamy, 188; © Travel Pictures/Alamy, 177; © Wayne
Hutchinson/Alamy, 201; © Will Watson/naturepl.com,
182–183

The information in this book is true and complete
to the best of our knowledge. All recommendations are
made without guarantee on the part of the author or
Storey Publishing. The author and publisher disclaim any
liability in connection with the use of this information.

Storey books are available for special premium and
promotional uses and for customized editions. For further
information, please call 1-800-793-9396.

Storey Publishing
210 MASS MoCA Way
North Adams, MA 01247
www.storey.com

Printed in China by Toppan Leefung Printing Ltd.
10 9 8 7 6 5 4 3 2 1

Library of Congress Cataloging-in-Publication Data
Smith, Beth, author, 1965–.
  The spinner's book of fleece / by Beth Smith.
    pages cm
  Includes index.
  ISBN 978-1-61212-039-3 (hardcover : alk. paper)
  ISBN 978-1-60342-875-0 (ebook) 1. Hand spinning.
  2. Wool. I. Title.
  TT847.S65 2014
  746.1'2—dc23
                                        2014008633

For my husband and best friend, Lou, who is the voice of reason to my nonsense and the calm in my whirlwind.

Contents

Foreword

This e-mail note from Beth Smith, written in 2008, captures perfectly the magic, enthusiasm, and wonder that she shares in this book.

> I teach a revolving breed study. Three months of fine wools, three months of long and crossbred wools, three months of Downy fibers, and three months of double-coated and "other" breeds. It's funny because I begin each introduction of a new breed with, "I love this wool. It's great for. . . ." The students think it's funny that I love them all.

Of course, I don't think that's at all funny! (Well, amusing: yes. Odd: no.) I, too, love the myriad and wonderful varieties of wool. Yet those multiple manifestations make it hard for fiber folk to get their minds (and hands) around the material and make the best use of each type.

To learn about and become confident in approaching and handling wool, you need curiosity and a plan. Many of us are in the position Beth was in before she began the serious work on this project, when she said, "I've spun samples for years and then never save them so have nothing to show for my work. Silly me." She began with curiosity and discovered the necessity for a plan (and some record-keeping).

To produce a guide like this requires much more. In addition to curiosity and a plan, it calls for enthusiasm, energy, determination, and perseverance, qualities Beth possesses in abundance. Moreover, she understands the allure of the prepared, hand-dyed braid (accompanied by the often unacknowledged need to understand the base fiber) and the potential confusion of being surrounded by dozens, possibly hundreds, of siren-calling fleeces at a festival.

Beth has bought literally hundreds of fleeces. She presents here a foundation and approach for exploring the different types, of putting them through their paces in a way that develops both familiarity and confidence, setting up good habits for working with any wool you may encounter. She also has opinions, which she's not afraid to share, always recognizing that they're hers. You, too, will develop opinions as you spin a wider variety of wools, one at a time (that's the best way: each on its own terms).

So turn the page and embark on the next phase of your own wool journey, with Beth as your guide. You're in good hands.

— DEBORAH ROBSON

Introduction
SPINNING WITH PURPOSE AND CONFIDENCE

"The sheep is of primary care of account if one has regard to the extent of its usefulness. For it is our principal protection against the violence of the cold and supplies us with a generous provision of coverings for our bodies. Then, too, it is the sheep which not only satisfies the hunger of the country folk with cheese and milk in abundance but also embellishes the tables of people of taste with a variety of agreeable dishes."
— Lucius Junius Moderatus Columella, *De Re Rustica (On Agriculture)*, 4 ce

In the not so distant past, people who wanted to spin their own yarn and did not own sheep had very limited options for fibers unless they were willing to do a lot of research and work to find a supplier. Merino for handspinners was very rare; Bluefaced Leicester was not readily available. Most of the wool that could be found was just labeled "wool" and was most likely a blend of a wide range of breeds. In recent years, the handspinning world has changed for the better, however, with more and more wool types available to handspinners, both processed and unwashed, right off the sheep ("in the grease"). Your options for making the perfect yarn for whatever project you have in mind are now wide open.

As the options expand, however, deciding which breed to choose can be confusing. Picture yourself in the fleece barn at a fiber festival. The selection can be extremely broad and varied, even within the same breed. Furthermore, you won't always know what breed you have in your hands. At some festivals, the fleeces are labeled only by the category they competed in, such as longwool, medium, or fine. And what about those very lovely fleeces you were given as a gift, which now are missing their labels? We all have wool, processed and unprocessed, that we neglected to label and have no idea what it is. Once you learn a few basic facts about the different types of wool and how to classify them, however, you will be able to work with the fibers you have in hand to make a project that is perfect for that particular wool.

AT LEFT: *A shawl using fleece from different sheep breeds to create the colored stripes is a great way to use small amounts spun while sampling. This shawl was designed by Lisa Jacobs for the Spinning Loft.*

The Method behind My Fleece Categories

In order to make processing and spinning decisions about fleeces, I look at crimp structure, lock shape, and relative fineness or coarseness, and put those with similar characteristics together. Usually these features are very easily determined by look and feel, so no special tools or testing are needed. Categorizing this way moves me toward the appropriate processing and spinning techniques that will result in the best yarn for the final product.

The great thing about categorizing wool by the way it looks before it's been washed or processed is that when you are out at that fiber festival or farm and you touch that most beautiful of fleeces, you can get an idea right away, before you even begin the washing process,

of how to use the wool and what kind of end product might suit it best. When the grease has been scoured out (washed), it sometimes becomes more difficult to evaluate the crimp structure. Seeing the dirty lock in the grease, therefore, is the perfect time to make decisions. You can feel confident that when you get it home, you will be able to process and spin that fleece into a yarn worthy of both the fantastic animal that produced it and the time it takes you, the artist, to create it.

I've grouped the breeds discussed here into five categories: fine wools, longwools, Down types, multicoats, and a few miscellaneous breeds. I describe the lock structure typical of each category, shown in a few pictures of the

Typical lock shapes of the four major breed categories.

(LEFT TO RIGHT) *Fine wool, longwool, Down/Down type, multicoat.*

breeds covered. Sometimes these descriptions are generalizations, because these are living animals whose wool may differ from animal to animal, fleece to fleece, region to region, and season to season. I've chosen breeds that represent the wide range and variety of wools available within a given category, so they are breeds that show the breadth within that category. Using the crimp and fiber diameters of these wools as a guide, you will be able to make wise decisions about how to handle the wools that are available to you or abundant in your area, even if they aren't the specific breeds I discuss here. Sometimes these decisions are judgment calls. After a bit of practice, for example, it's easy to see that Lincoln belongs in the long-wools category. A wool such as Polypay, however, may not look like a fine wool to everyone.

My choices were also determined by what breeds are available to me. Most of the fleeces come from sheep that were raised in the United States. Although more than a thousand sheep breeds exist worldwide, it is, unfortunately, almost impossible to get samples of all of them. We do, however, now have access to more than one hundred breeds in the United States alone; if you live in another part of the world, your choices may be different. The benefit of this book is that you don't have to spin the actual breeds I am talking about. You can compare the characteristics of the fleece you have to a similar breed that is covered here and feel confident that you can successfully work with it using a similar approach. (For more about fleece characteristics, see chapter 2 and descriptions of each category in chapters 4 through 8.)

The Problem with Medium

Many people refer to certain wool types as medium wools. I have not included a category called "medium" here, because I feel it isn't descriptive enough and doesn't give any clues about how to handle it. The word *medium* could include possibly hundreds of breeds and gives no information about the properties of the wool beyond a vague description of its fiber diameter, often described in terms of micron measurement or Bradford count. The problem is that although different breeds may have fibers with similar measurements, their fleeces may scream to be treated differently to show off their best assets.

Micron measurement is the average diameter of a fiber sample measured in microns, usually with computer imaging, but in the past a microscope was the most common measuring tool. The expressed measurement is an average of the fibers in the sample. (For more about micron measurements and wool grading, see page 79.)

Bradford count is a measurement of how many 560-yard skeins of singles yarn can theoretically be spun from 1 pound of top. For example, if the fibers are described as 44s, it means that forty-four 560-yard hanks of singles could be spun from that fiber. From finer wools, such as Merino, you may get as many as 80 skeins, and from coarser wools, as few as 36.

Discovering Hidden Beauty

As you explore each category covered in these pages, you'll notice that handspinners and mills alike often find some reason to dismiss a breed type as not useful or desirable. (The exception to this is probably the fine wools.) If you stick with me, however, I hope to help you see the usefulness of each, and inspire you to try them all. Of course, not all wools are good for all things, but there is a use for each one. Even in situations where you may not be sure of the best way to spin and use a wool, you'll learn to sample and try each fleece in different ways until its beauty and strong points shine through.

I often refer to some wools as suitable for next-to-skin wear. When I say this, I'm usually thinking of skin on more sensitive places like necks and foreheads — those places on my own body that are most sensitive to the "prickle factor." I wouldn't generally make a hat out of a strong wool such as Lincoln, which is on the high end of micron measurements. But I would have no issue using the same wool for a cardigan sweater that I'll be wearing over another top. I would probably also be willing to use middle-of-the-road and stronger wools for socks. They would certainly last longer, and my ankles aren't as sensitive as my neck. It's not necessarily essential to use the finer wools for those kinds of projects.

Making a Strong Case

Different words mean different things to different people. The word *coarse* seems to make many people think scratchy or harsh when it comes to wool. For this reason, I like to use the word *strong*. I first heard it used in this way by wool expert and teacher Deborah Robson; it's been with me ever since.

Just because a wool has a higher micron count than another does not automatically relegate it to the world of rugs. Strong wools such as Lincoln and Teeswater do make beautiful rugs, but they can also be used to make delicate lace and elegant garments.

All Breeds Deserve a Second Chance

Certain shepherds have supplied me with fleeces for many years, and so I've seen the effect that extreme heat or drought, unusual cold, stressful weather, sickness, or even lambing can have on the fleece of the same sheep from year to year. Because of this experience I urge you not to dismiss the wool of an entire breed due to one bad experience, and show you how to look at a fleece and make good, informed decisions about the best approach for your project (see Digging Deeper, page 29). You'll see how to take the good things into account (a lock that "sings" to you), as well as things to avoid (staple lengths unsuited for your purpose). You'll find out how to judge the seriousness of potential problems, such as breaks, scurf, fiber weakness, vegetable matter, poor skirting, and uncoated fleeces. Just as important, you'll discover that some things that may scare you off aren't really that scary after all.

Start from Scratch or Buy Processed Wool?

Many of you who have washed and processed wool may be thinking, "Been there, done that, not going back." Although you may change your mind about this after learning about the simple processing methods I use, you may still feel you just don't have the space or time to manage raw fleece. Don't worry. My categorizations can also provide guidance when you find that luscious braid of the most perfect color of processed wool. It may take a little more sleuthing, but you can look at that wool and make educated decisions that help you make the yarn you want for the specific project you have in mind.

There are times when all of us want to sit down with a braid of fiber and just spin for the pure enjoyment that comes with spinning. It's good to do that sometimes. Spin it and decide what to do with it later. But for those times when you have that most precious of fibers, that most beautiful of fleeces, or a whole bunch of one fiber, spinning with a purpose in mind will bring real satisfaction.

I had several goals in mind when writing this book. The first and most obvious is to show spinners all that is possible to do with a wool just by combining a variety of preparation techniques with a range of spinning methods. Because the kinds of yarns you can spin are endless, what I illustrate here is just a taste. Second, but maybe more important, I hope to help spinners learn to try things just for the joy of experimentation, to get beyond worrying about doing

it "wrong," and to stop thinking that they will somehow ruin the wool. In my spinning life, I've had an abundance of yarns gone wrong, but those accidents have taught me more than I have ever learned from my "successes." So come with me and work your way through this book, and if yarns happen that you don't like, well then, try again. The sheep are, after all, growing more wool as we speak!

It's hard to resist the beautifully dyed batts, top, and roving that one encounters at yarn stores and fiber festivals.

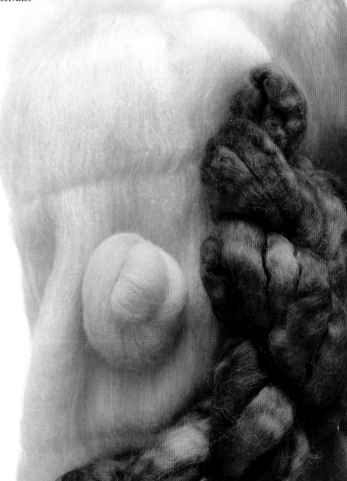

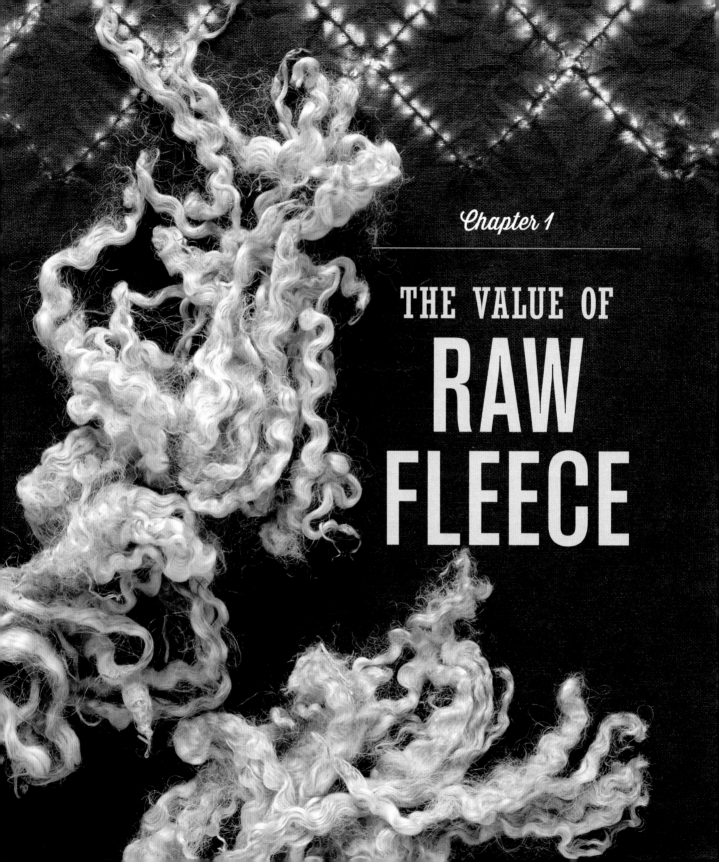

Chapter 1

THE VALUE OF
RAW
FLEECE

I BEGAN KNITTING because there were things I wanted that I couldn't find in the store. I began spinning because I was curious about where yarn comes from. I continued spinning prepared fiber from a mill because I realized that I could make yarns I couldn't find in the store. Preparing your own fiber from raw fleece takes that exploration one step further.

Many of the fibers included in this book can readily be found in both raw and processed forms, but I am a huge proponent of processing your own fibers from scratch. I have several reasons for this. The first is that by doing the prep yourself by hand, you'll often get a more consistent yarn. The second is that commercial processors sometimes use harsh detergents and other chemicals to remove vegetable matter (VM) and other forms of dirt from fibers, and these chemicals can affect the texture of the fleece. This makes the finished yarn a bit less soft and sometimes not as lustrous as a yarn spun from fleece that has been hand processed under gentler conditions. This drawback is particularly true of fleece from large mills that process hundreds and even thousands of pounds of the same wool types at a time. It's not usually a problem, however, with fleece from small local mills that accept batches of fiber as small as one fleece.

A third reason to process your own wool is that you can choose a particular fleece that will work for your particular project. As mentioned earlier, the qualities of several fleeces, although from the same breed, can be different from region to region, from farm to farm, and even from sheep to sheep. The Romney fleece I get from a local flock in the Midwest may have similar characteristics to a fleece acquired in the West, but the hand, or feel, of the wool may change. A lamb's fleece from that same midwestern Romney flock may be perfect for making scarves and hats, while the fleece of an adult ewe from the same flock is crying out to be a cardigan or even a lovely rug for the kitchen.

A Consistent Yarn: Fantasy or Possibility?

Many modern sheep breeds that are used mainly for their wool have been bred for consistency of fleece. This means the fibers from the neck of the sheep will be similar in fiber diameter, crimp structure, and lock length to the fibers taken from the side or back end of the same animal. This makes machine processing easier and also predictable from one lot to the next.

Completely mechanical spinning machines were developed to imitate what human hands could do. When we handspin with a view to spinning the perfect yarn, we're not trying to copy what machines can do or what can be bought in a store. Instead, we're trying to be the best spinners we can be. Although this may not be every spinner's goal, if you are someone who took up the craft of spinning for this reason, know that very smooth, consistent yarn is an achievable goal that will come with time and focused practice.

All handspun yarns, from delicate to novelty, will make beautiful fabrics. Which will be best for the purpose depends on your goals.

Skirting and Sorting Matters

Hopefully, the fleece has been skirted before you buy it. *Skirting* not only removes dung tags and lots of stained areas around the outside of the fleece, it also removes the belly wool and neck wool that generally has the most VM. With many breeds, however, some wool consisting of different lengths and textures remains after skirting, and this is where sorting comes in.

Corriedales and Merinos are examples of sheep that have been bred to have a very consistent fleece all over their bodies. This means that the lock length and crimp is similar from head to tail, and the fleece will easily make a similar yarn regardless of where the wool is taken from the body. On the other hand, more primitive breeds, such as Jacob and Shetland, have a range of different fiber diameters, crimps, and staple lengths (lock length) on different parts of the body. The wool on an animal's shoulders is generally softest, possibly getting coarser as you move from front to back. In their book *In Sheep's Clothing,* Nola and Jane Fournier write that there may be up to 14 different types of wool on one sheep, depending on the breed and her age.

Sorting your wool before processing it may help you avoid spinning an inconsistent yarn that is the result of dealing with different fiber lengths and degrees of coarseness. Sorting also helps prevent getting a yarn with different rates of shrinkage caused by differing amounts of crimp in fibers from different parts of the sheep, as well as a yarn that accepts dye unevenly because the different wool textures take the dye differently.

Is it always necessary to sort the fleece before spinning? In my opinion the answer is no, not always. It depends on how special the item is that you will be making, how much wool you need for your project, and how much blending you plan to do with it before you spin it. If you will be carding the fleece, you can card the coarser wool from the rump with the softer wools from the shoulders and sides to make a more homogenous yarn that will be consistent throughout the project.

It's a Woman's World . . . Sort Of

Most wool that you purchase will have come from a ewe, which is why throughout this book I refer to the sheep as "her." Most flocks are made up of almost all ewes with just a small number of rams kept around for breeding season. This is not to say that wool from a ram isn't good wool, but because ewes vastly outnumber rams in the large flocks, the chances that the fleece you are getting is from a ewe are high.

Generally speaking, wool from a ram will have a bit stronger odor than a ewe fleece and will also be a bit coarser. As with everything in spinning, however, generalizations aren't always accurate. I have had many ram fleeces that were beautiful and wonderful to work with. Don't discount a fleece because it is from a ram, but do make sure it will work for your purposes.

Going by Feel

When you buy a fleece, it will sometimes be folded and rolled after the skirting. The two sides are folded into the center, then the back end is rolled toward the front, and finally the neck wool is stretched out a bit and used to wrap around and secure the fleece. When you unroll the fleece to look at it, make sure you remember which part was wrapped around it, so you can distinguish the front end from the back. Sometimes you can see the different wool qualities, but mostly you will be going by feel. As I said, not all breeds exhibit big differences in the characteristics of various parts of one fleece, so if you think it all will work well together, don't worry about it.

If, on the other hand, you find that some of the wool won't work for the soft sweater you have in mind, you can always put the coarser wool aside to use in rugs or bags or even as stuffing. All wool has a purpose.

The fleece from "Copper," a California Variegated Mutant/Romeldale cross, has been skirted and laid out so that you can identify the various parts: (1) *neck;* (2) *front legs;* (3) *chest (usually removed when skirted);* (4) *belly (usually removed when skirted);* (5) *rear legs;* (6) *rump;* (7) *shoulders;* (8) *back.*

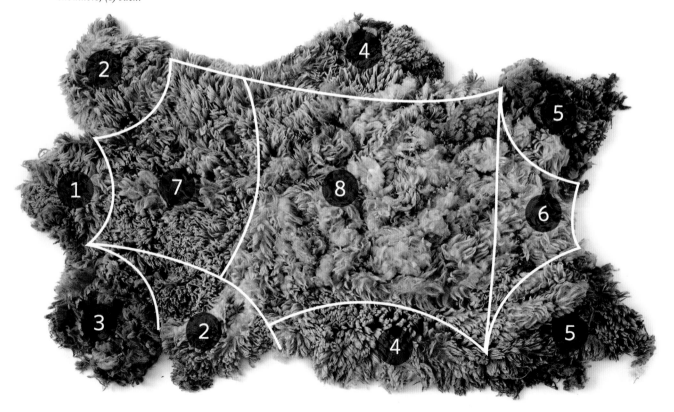

An Introduction to Hand Scouring

There are many different ways to wash fleeces (usually referred to as *scouring*), but what I describe here is what works best for me and my purposes and also avoids tragic felting mistakes. I give detailed washing information for each breed category, though the washing methods are similar from one category to another.

My methods are specifically for small-scale scouring. I wash fleeces in small batches of about 8 to 24 ounces at a time, depending on the size container I'm using. When choosing a container, it's important that there be plenty of water around the fibers so that the dirt and grease has plenty of room to move away from the wool. For years, I washed fleece in ordinary kitchen dishpans that hold about 2½ gallons of water comfortably (before fleece is added). These pans accommodate about 8 ounces of a high-volume fleece, such as a Down type. I now use larger containers that hold about 4½ gallons of water before I add the fleece, so that I can wash 1 to 1½ pounds of fleece in them.

I prefer somewhat shallow, flexible containers, sometimes called *trugs*, which are available at feed, hardware, and garden stores. Their flexibility and convenient handles make it easy to empty the water without removing the fleece and still control the fleece from escaping into the sink. These containers are also easy to move from one spot to another, since I generally work with multiple containers at the same time. I have three containers and a counter next to my sink, so I can wash up to 4½ pounds of fleece in about 2 hours. For many breeds of sheep that means a whole skirted fleece can be done without too much hard work and without water up to my elbows.

You'll need to experiment with washing techniques, especially to ascertain what works in your water. City water differs from well water, and well water is different from place to place, depending on whether it's hard or soft. The water itself doesn't necessarily affect the outcome, but your detergent and the way it reacts with the minerals in your water can have a big effect on how clean a fleece gets.

I always use a wool scour that was formulated specifically for removing lanolin from wool. Though such a scour may seem more expensive than detergents and soaps you can get at the local grocery store, the amount required to scour the wool is much less than the amount of household cleaner needed. I've tried almost all of the scouring agents on the market, and my preferred wool scour is Unicorn Power Scour, made by Unicorn Fibre. Other experienced fiber people recommend other detergents, but Power Scour is the one I find consistently gives me great results, regardless of the fleece's grease content. It can be used at lower temperatures than the other scours (which means no boiling water is necessary), and I use a fraction of the amount required by other detergents I've tried.

In a pinch, household dish soap also works and may seem like a less expensive way to go. In order to remove the grease, however, it's important to use enough soap so that the water feels slippery, and it may not be as inexpensive as you think. In addition, soap creates quite a lot of suds, which means you'll need many rinses to remove the soap. In contrast, Unicorn Power Scour cuts down on the amount of rinse water required by at least a third.

The final word is experiment! Try every recommended method that you come across and discover what works best for you. I've made many mistakes and lost some fleece to tragic errors, but I rarely experiment with more than a pound at a time, so my losses are minimal. Once, I put a whole fleece in the washing machine, and another time a whole fleece in the bathtub. While neither experience felted those fleeces, they made me realize that I wasn't comfortable working with more than 1 to 2 pounds at a time. Experimenting with various washing and prep methods resulted in the approach I use now, and I'm very comfortable with the whole process.

How Clean Is Clean?

Although the tips of your fleece may not look completely clean after scouring, they will open up during the fiber prep step, and anything that looks like dirt will be gone with whichever processing method you choose. Be aware that certain breeds produce bright white fleeces, whereas the "white" fleeces of other breeds may appear more off-white or even yellow. If your problem is stains, however, you'll find that these aren't necessarily easy to get rid of. Yellow in color, a canary stain, for instance, will not wash out, although it does not affect

the strength of the fiber. (For more information about canary stains, see page 31.) If staining is your problem, sometimes overdyeing is the only solution.

Keep in mind that the final rinse may not run completely clear. Your main goal at this point is to remove the lanolin so that the fibers move freely past each other during spinning. You don't have to get out every bit of dirt during this initial scouring, because you'll wash the skeins after spinning, as well as after finishing whatever you make with your yarn. By then, all of the dirt will be gone.

Don't Overestimate VM

The sad fact is that no amount of washing will get out all of the vegetable matter — VM. But VM is not the end of the world. Some can be picked or shaken out before scouring. Still more will come out in the wash, and even more will come out in the processing, especially if you are using combs or a flick card. And then the spinning and plying allows more to fall out or for larger bits to be picked out. Don't write off a good fleece due to a little barnyard dirt. You'd be dirty, too, if you had to wear the same clothes for six months to a year!

Of course there are those fleeces with teeny, tiny ground-up bits of hay, and there might be more than you would like to deal with. So, if it is a breed type you are likely to see frequently, it's okay to pass by the dirtier ones. But for those rare occasions you stumble upon a rare breed, don't be afraid of VM.

Storing Raw Fleece and Processed Fiber

You can store fleece for years. Over time, the grease will harden a bit, but hot water will come to the rescue. If stored well in an appropriate container, you should have no worries. Good containers include cloth bags, such as pillowcases or canvas sacks. Paper bags also work, as do dry-cleaner bags meant for storing bedding. Any of these options should protect the fleece from moths, but if the fleece happens to be contaminated, other fibers stored in the same area will be protected if you keep them separate in appropriate containers. Plastic bags are not optimal for long-term storage. Wool is always trading moisture with the air around it, and plastic traps the moisture, possibly resulting in mold or mildew problems. Large plastic containers are usually not airtight, so the worry about mold or mildew isn't really a concern.

Processed fibers can get compacted and matted over time, so it's better to give them a bit of space no matter what way you decide to store them. I like plastic containers as a quarantine measure, but if you have the room, open shelving is best. Moths don't like light or fresh air; they love dark corners. Optimally, your fibers will be stored in a well-lit place with lots of room for air to circulate around it. If this isn't possible, then the next best thing is to go through your stash frequently and move things around often.

An Overview of Fiber-Prep Tools

Before I go into specifics about fiber prep tools, I'd like to climb onto my soapbox for a moment here and talk about tools in general. I encourage you to get the best tools your budget allows. Many people use pet-grooming tools as an inexpensive alternative to tools built specifically for fiber preparation (see Using Dog-Grooming Tools, page 214). Although these give you an idea of how real fiber-prep tools work, they don't give you the true results. There really is a difference between just using two dog slickers in contrast to handcards made with carding cloth designed specifically for wool.

Tools made specifically for wool processing provide the results you're looking for in less time and with less effort than do other options. Although they may seem expensive, properly cared-for wool-processing tools will last for many years. I have seen 25-year-old handcards that are still usable. I purchased my favorite set of handcombs used, at least 10 years ago. Bang for the buck, it's much better to spend more money at the start and have tools that will last a lifetime, as opposed to buying tools that need to be replaced on a regular basis because the pins can't stand up to the stress that fiber prep puts on them.

I always recommend trying any tools before you buy. This includes everything from spindles to flicks, hand combs, and spinning wheels. In my perfect world, there would be a spinning supply store in every town. Sadly, we aren't there yet, so while we wait for that to happen, many of us will have to take a few risks in the tool-buying department.

When you're making buying decisions, it's good to go with tools that have a solid reputation and have worked for other spinners you know. This method of purchasing may mean that you will have to order two or more different brands or styles until you find one that fits your hands, body, or style. The good news is that there is a thriving network for used tools on the Internet, including several websites devoted to selling just fiber tools (see resources on page 239 for suggestions).

Worsted and Woolen SPINNING BASICS

The techniques for prepping and spinning wool span a wide spectrum. At one extreme is the approach known as woolen; at the other extreme is worsted. The schools of thought about each of these are just as far apart. The methods I offer here are based on my experience and research on these topics. Most of us spin yarn that's something in the middle of true woolen and true worsted, and we're happy with our results, but it's good to understand the terms and know how to get to the extremes when you want.

Worsted yarn. A true worsted yarn is hand-combed with all of the fibers aligned and all of the butts and tips of each fiber facing the same way. After handcombing, which removes all the shortest fibers, the fiber is pulled through the hole of a tool called a *diz*, forming combed top. (See Using a Diz, page 118.) The top is spun, taking care to keep either the butt or the tip moving in the same direction for the entire length of the singles yarn. During the spinning, twist is not allowed to enter the fiber supply, with the result that very little air is trapped between the fibers. The purpose of the worsted technique is to smooth and compact the fibers to make a dense yarn with some luster or a smooth finish. Because little air is trapped in the yarn, garments made with it are not as warm as those made with a woolen-spun yarn. This makes worsted yarn a good choice for a warm-weather sweater.

Spinning worsted style

Some tools take a lot of practice in order to perfect the technique. In-person lessons are the best choice and the fastest way to success in these cases. There are also online sources for videos and instruction that can get you on your way until that in-person class is available. Different instructors use different techniques, so don't give up if that first try doesn't get you where you want to be.

Wheels or Spindles?

Most of the techniques described in this book can be done with any spinning wheel or hand-spindle. I don't describe drafting methods in depth, beyond defining woolen- and worsted-spun (see Worsted and Woolen Spinning Basics, below). The twist in woolen-spun yarns is allowed to enter the fiber supply, whereas the twist in worsted-spun yarns is not allowed into

I don't consider mill-prepared top to be a true worsted preparation. It will result in a nice smooth yarn, but because the fibers are carded first and all of the tips and cut ends aren't facing the same direction, it is one step down from a true worsted prep.

Woolen yarn. In a true woolen yarn, the fibers are carded and then rolled into a rolag (see page 159) and spun from the end. Because the fibers are rolled up in the rolag, they come out of the fiber supply in a spiraling pattern, sideways to the orifice. This means that in the yarn, those fibers sit a bit sideways, pushing out against each other and thus creating air pockets. This true woolen yarn is spun using a technique known as *long draw*, which allows the twist to enter the fiber supply and grab the fibers as it does so. The spinner controls the thickness of the yarn by managing the amount of twist. This airy yarn has great insulating properties.

Both worsted and woolen yarns have their own strengths and also their own drawbacks. It

is up to the spinner to decide what end result he or she would like for the intended project. In chapters 4 through 8, I discuss the fiber-prep technique that I feel is best suited to the wools in each category, but then I explain how multiple drafting techniques change the resulting yarn. Even though few of us spin true woolen or true worsted yarn, we can use combinations of woolen and worsted prep and spinning techniques to change the outcome and get a yarn that is perfect for what we want.

Spinning woolen style

the fiber supply. This means that these yarns, and anything on the spectrum in between, can be spun on a spindle or a spinning wheel. It also doesn't matter whether your wheel is Irish tension, Scotch tension, or double drive. Although those drive systems can make a difference in your yarns, I'm not dealing with those differences in the context of this book.

Your Choice Matters

The main purpose of any style of fiber preparation is to straighten and align the fibers, and to open the tips to make the spinning easier. Your decision about which tool to use to accomplish this is based on the end result you would like reflected in your yarn. For instance, handcards and drumcarders do align fibers, but combing aligns them to a greater extent. The carding process doesn't remove short fiber, and when you card, you aren't trying to keep butts and tips heading in the same direction. If you spin worsted yarn, you take pains to keep the alignment combing provides. In contrast, when you spin a woolen yarn from carded fibers, you do your best to preserve the air you've built in by spinning from rolags or by spinning long draw so that air is trapped by the twist.

Next, I will give you an overview of wool-preparation tools. A description of how to use each one is covered in subsequent chapters according to fleece category.

Flick Cards

A flick card, also known as a flicker, is designed to open the fibers in each lock of wool. This is one of the least expensive tools you can purchase for fiber preparation, and you can use it for almost any wool. I say *almost* any because the longer-stapled (meaning longer lock length) longwools may be a bit difficult to open in the center of the lock. In addition, any wool that has a staple length of less than 3 inches may be difficult to flick without drawing blood, because it's hard to get your fingers out of the way enough and still maintain a strong grip on the lock.

Several toolmakers make great flicks. The working end of the tool, where the cloth is attached, may be rectangular or square, and flat or curved. The rectangle may be positioned either horizontally or vertically on the handle. The cloth may have anywhere from 36 to 72 pins per square inch, sometimes more, depending on which brand you choose. Which flick you choose is completely personal. If you have an opportunity to try out a few, do so. The handle should feel comfortable, and you should be able to hold it without having it spin around in your hand. As for the carding cloth, almost any will do the job. A finer cloth will do the job a bit faster, but possibly with a bit more waste.

I can't say that the prep from a flick card is completely worsted, though I consider it more worsted than woolen. The fact that the short fibers may not be completely removed makes yarns spun from flicked locks a bit fluffier than if the locks were combed and dizzed (see Making Top after Combing, page 118, for more about the diz). To me, yarn spun from a flicked prep resembles that from a combed prep that is removed from the combs without using a diz to pull it through. (For detailed information about flick-card techniques, see pages 72–74.)

FLICK CARDS

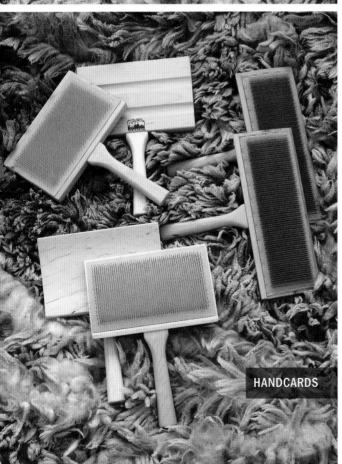

HANDCARDS

Waste Not, Want Not?

If you're worried about having more waste when you use a fine-tooth carding cloth, don't be. The drawback of more waste is obvious — more wasted fiber. The benefit of more waste, however, is that short bits, weak fibers, and knots are removed. Getting these out of your fleece before you spin means you can make a more consistent yarn.

Handcards

Many companies make handcards, so here's a rundown of a few things to consider when making a decision about which ones to buy.

Comfort. At the top of the list of requirements is comfort. The handle shape is a big factor in whether you can work with the cards for a good length of time. Some cards have flat, thin handles, some have a flatter handle that widens, and some have a handle that is almost round. Part of the deciding factor about handle shape is what carding method you use. If you hold your cards almost at the bed (the working part covered with the carding cloth) and stabilize the cards by placing your fingers over the back of the bed, then the round handles will be just fine. If you hold the handles farther back and wrap your hand completely around the handle, then you might want the stability that a flattened handle provides.

Weight. Each manufacturer uses a different wood for their cards. Although you want a hard wood that is going to stand up to years of use, you also want cards that are a comfortable weight. The best way to know this is to hold them in your hand. Because most of us don't live near a shop with a variety of handcards in stock, it may be difficult to evaluate them in person. If that's the case, fiber festivals and shows are your friends. There you'll find many vendors with handcards that you can hold and evaluate. Failing that, check the resources (page 239) for a list of manufacturers, then phone, e-mail, or check the manufacturer's website to find out the nearest supplier. You may also get advice at your local fiber store.

Back shape. In addition to choosing the handle and weight that's right for you, you have a choice of cards with curved or flat backs. I'll say right out front that I am a curved-cards girl. I use them for everything. I've never loved flat cards, but I have friends who strongly prefer them and would fight to the death to keep them. People generally love what they learned on. The carding technique (described in detail in chapter 6) is a bit different depending on which type you have.

Pins per square inch. Your final decision is how many pins per square inch (psi) of carding cloth to choose. This number can be anywhere from as few as 54 psi all the way to 248 psi. Cards with somewhere between 70 and 112 psi are the most common; most cotton cards have more than 200 psi. You may sometimes see "pins per square inch" referred to as "teeth per inch" (tpi).

If this is your first set of handcards, it's best to get a set that cards a wide range of fibers. If you love the finer wools and process them the most, then 72 psi will work, but 112 psi will get the job done with fewer passes. If you have no preference for a specific wool and want to process the whole range of fibers, then 72s might be the cards for you. Many of us who process pounds and pounds of fleece have collected several sets of handcards so that we can match the tool with the fleece or specific fiber we are carding.

Though in this book the focus is on processing raw fleece, handcards will also serve you well for blending both different fibers and different colors, and so they will come in handy for a long time for a variety of purposes. (For detailed handcarding information, see pages 155–61.)

Drumcarders

Drumcarders are used to achieve results similar to what you get using handcards, but on a larger scale. Whereas handcards hold about 0.1 to 0.2 ounce of wool, a home-size drumcarder can usually hold 1 to 2 ounces at a time, depending on the size of the main drum and the length of the teeth on the carding cloth.

This doesn't mean that a drumcarder is always faster than handcarding. With practice, someone using handcards can process similar amounts of wool as fast as, or even faster than, using a drumcarder built for home use. This is because it takes time to load the fiber for the first pass so it doesn't clump. Furthermore, turning the crank, at least for the first pass, should be done very slowly to avoid getting noils (little knots of fiber). In addition, when you are working with certain fine wools, you need to turn slowly *every* pass because of the wool's tendency to snap back, which is what causes those little knots in the first place.

DRUMCARDERS

If you decide to purchase a drumcarder, here are a few things to take into consideration: pins per square inch, type of licker-in, storage requirements, need for multiple drums, and electric or hand cranked. Additional drums further smooth and align the fiber, which results in fewer passes to fully prepare the fiber in each batt. Drumcarders with three or more drums are usually electric. If you're buying your first carder, however, I don't recommend either a multiple drum or an electric model. Removing these two items from the equation brings the cost down considerably. The best way to decide among drumcarders is to try them out with the fibers you are likely to use the most.

Size of drum. Drumcarders come in a variety of sizes. Larger ones usually have a bigger main drum, allowing you to make larger batts. If your plan is to process only one or two fleeces a year, as well as do some color and fiber blending, a smaller, more portable carder will be just fine, again lowering the cost.

Licker-in and carding cloth. In addition to the main drum, drumcarders have a licker-in, which is a smaller drum that sits in front of the larger one and pulls the fiber in. The cloth on the licker-in is generally covered in a carding cloth with fewer pins per inch than the main drum. Sometimes the licker-in has sharp, knife-like teeth, instead of pin-style teeth. Which type you choose is personal. If the drum of your licker-in has regular carding cloth, you should expect to lose some fiber to it. Once the licker-in fills with fiber, it won't pick up any more, so, to keep waste down, don't clean the licker-in between batches of the same fiber.

COMBS

Combs

For worsted fiber preparation, combs are what you want. Although there is a wide variety of comb types and sizes, the techniques for using them are pretty similar, except for the Russian paddle combs, which I discuss on this page. The rows of tines on a comb are also referred to as *pitch*. A one-row comb, for example, is called single pitch; a comb with two rows is a 2-pitch comb, and so on. Here is a rundown of your options.

❶ Mini combs. Mini combs are just that — small, handheld combs. The size of mini combs can vary greatly from one manufacturer to the next. Most have only one or two rows of tines.

❷ Viking combs are also handheld, but they are a bit larger than mini combs. They may have one, two, or three rows of tines. Like the mini combs, they are small enough to hold and use without a clamp, but you can process more fiber at a time with them.

❸ English combs. The combs in a pair of English combs match, but one is generally put in a clamping device to anchor it to a table or other stable surface, while the other comb does the work. Both have handles and are generally between 3 and 5 pitch. The fibers are transferred back and forth between the combs using the handheld comb.

❹ Dutch combs have one or two rows of tines. One comb has a handle, and the other, which is clamped to a table, does not. The tines on these combs are wider set, so they are better for coarser wools.

❺ Russian paddle combs. These combs are very wide, with finer and shorter tines than on the other comb types and, traditionally, with only a single row. This design evolved because the wool available in the area of the world where these combs were developed was double coated, and these combs made it easy to separate the coats. Once separated, the finer undercoat was spun right from the comb into a very fine yarn. Today's manufacturers are making Russian paddle combs with two rows, to accommodate the wide range of fibers now available to handspinners. To use a Russian paddle comb, place one comb on a peg to hold it stationary. Come straight down on the stationary comb with the other, pull the fiber straight out to the front, and then spin right off the comb.

Russian paddle combs are generally used when you're preparing to spin fine yarn. They aren't great all-around combs, however, so they're not a good choice if you're just learning to comb. On the other hand, if you have some experience with spinning and fiber prep and know that very fine spinning is what you love, then these combs can be perfect.

Choosing Which Combs to Buy

Except for Russian paddle combs, you'll find that the process of combing is very similar from one to the next. You either comb while holding both combs, or you stabilize one comb and work with the other. In every case, the combs are perpendicular to each other while you comb. (For more information about the combing technique, see Combing the Longwools, pages 112–121.)

Start small when you buy your first pair of combs. A set of handheld 2-pitch combs can be an affordable way to begin combing. Most people who enjoy worsted fiber prep have two or more sets of combs: one set for all-around prep (the original combs) and another set for specializing with the wool types and yarns they love to spin.

For my all-around handheld combs, I like a set with two rows of tines of about medium thickness, set not too close together. The pair I own is comfortable in my hand and isn't too heavy. I've been using it for 10 years and expect to be using it for at least another 15 years for sampling, experimenting, combing small amounts, and spinning right from the comb.

Neps and Noils and VM . . . Oh My!

Neps are imperfections caused by fibers that are immature or haven't been straightened properly.

Noils are waste and knots of wool that may happen during processing.

VM is vegetable matter — grain, grass, weeds, and so on — that the animal picked up in the field.

For specialty combs, I suggest getting a set with multiple rows of tines. If you prefer to do most of your fiber prep all at one time or plan to process more than one fleece per year, then 4- to 5-pitch combs are fantastic. The more rows of tines on the combs, the more neps, noils, VM, and short fibers you can remove with each pass. More tines, therefore, means less work for each comb load. A 5-pitch comb helps to process that entire fleece in what will feel like record time if you are used to double-pitch handheld combs.

Combs with one of the pair clamped are also useful, because you can then hold the free comb with both hands, making it feel lighter and easier to maneuver. It also makes removing fiber with a diz more convenient, because you can use both hands for the task, without worrying about holding onto the comb. (For information on how to use a diz, see Making Top after Combing, page 118.)

As with other tools, try some different types of combs, if possible. Maybe members of your spinning and weaving guild have examples of various types, or your local fiber store may carry a variety. Ask other spinners what they have and what they love. Used combs don't come around very often, but this is a good option for a bit of savings. However, savings in the short run may not be savings over time if you don't like the tool, and it sits unused.

A Spinner's ESSENTIAL TOOLS

The only really essential spinning equipment is fiber and a spinning tool, like a handspindle or a spinning wheel. But we all like some extras, and there are lots of bits and bobs you can buy. Here are the things I keep near me when I am spinning.

- **Correct wrenches or tools** for quick wheel tune-ups. These include an Allen wrench (if your wheel needs one) that fits your wheel and/or a short-handled screwdriver that's easy to pack when you're spinning away from home.

- **Oil.** This truly is an essential for most wheels. Wheels with sealed bearings don't need general oiling, but even so, the bobbin shaft always needs lubrication. I use 30-weight motor oil for almost all of my oiling, which is recommended by most major wheel manufacturers. Check your manual or ask your dealer to make sure. White lithium grease also works very well on the bobbin shaft. It can be a great choice for hinges, too, since it doesn't drip.

- **Medium handcards.** The ones with 72 psi will do all kinds of fibers.

- **Medium handcombs.** These will comb almost anything from fine to coarse fleeces.

- **Flick, flicker, flick carder.** Three names for the same tool! The least expensive processing tool you can buy, and it works on almost any fleece.

- **Hang tags.** I always have some of these for labeling both spun and unspun samples. I also like to carry them at fiber festivals for anything I buy that needs a label. Surveyor's flagging tape also works well because it's waterproof, so your sample can keep its tag even when it goes for a soak.

- **Permanent marker** for labeling things.

- **Orifice hook.** I sometimes go without, but the hook gets the job done faster.

Chapter 2

BUYING A FLEECE:
DOs AND DON'Ts

YOU WALK INTO THE FLEECE BARN. You are there with all of the fleeces in front of you. They are beautiful. There's a frenzy of buying. You need to get yours. The color is beautiful. It looks pretty good in the bag, and so you bring it home. . . .

I've done this a million times. Well, maybe not a million, but plenty. And some of those plenty times I have been not as happy with my purchase as I had hoped. I've learned a lot. I do sometimes get caught up in the auction moment or the grabbing time but not as often as I used to. So let's talk about the things we want to see in any fleece and also how to decide on the fleeces sitting in front of you at a festival or a shearing.

The first thing I think about before I buy a fleece for my own use is what I want to use it for. This saves me from getting caught up in the moment and buying a fleece that I don't necessarily need. Am I looking for a fleece to knit a cardigan that I will wear over a shirt? Do I want something to throw on and lounge in? Do I want to weave fabric for a skirt? Do I want a warm shawl, or a delicate lace one? Something smooth or with a fuzzy halo? These are the kinds of questions I ask myself before I touch a fleece; otherwise I'm likely to be overwhelmed. I still make mistakes when I buy, and I use these mistakes as learning experiences. Most fleeces are very affordable and a relatively small investment will bring a large amount of learning, experience, and spinning pleasure.

Deciding How Much to Buy

It can be a little difficult to decide how much wool to buy. When you buy at fiber festivals and farms, you generally need to buy the entire fleece. This isn't always a bad thing, because you can get a whole fleece for not a lot of money this way. If you have only a scarf in mind, however, a whole fleece may not be right for you. In that case, check out retailers who specialize in fleece and sell in smaller quantities. This not only avoids being overwhelmed by a 10-pound Cormo fleece, but it also allows you to sample lots of breeds to help you figure out what works best for your project before putting a lot of time and effort into a wool that may not actually be suited to the purpose you have in mind.

Remember that a fleece will lose between 30 and 50 percent of its weight in the scouring, as the dirt and grease in it fall away. It is also good to factor in a loss of an additional 10 percent for waste in processing. This figure is a bit high, but better safe than sorry. You don't want to run out of wool for your project, and because there are no dye lots for raw fleece to search for on the Internet, it's better to be sure and get enough the first time.

Here are some numbers I keep in my head when I'm in this situation:

- **For mittens or a hat,** 4 ounces of scoured wool is usually enough.

- **For a solid-knit scarf,** 6 to 8 ounces of scoured wool will generally work.

- **For a vest,** figure 12 to 16 ounces of scoured wool.

- **For a cardigan or pullover,** you'll need 16 to 24 ounces of scoured wool.

These numbers are generally for knit items. For weaving, I would stick with numbers that are about the same, for safety's sake; for crochet, you may need quite a bit more. These numbers should be adjusted, depending on whether your design is lace, cable, or stranded colorwork, or stockinette stitch, plain weave, or overshot. Patterns with more layers of yarns, such as overshot or cables, for example, are heavier and need more materials. I also always add another 2 to 4 ounces for sampling.

The Value of Touch

It's good to touch and get acquainted in person with the particular fleece you are buying, unless you have a relationship with an individual shepherd or a history of buying from a particular online or mail-order source and therefore trust them to help you choose. It can be difficult to discern the various characteristics of a fleece from a photo, especially if you are new to buying unprepared wool. Even those of us who have been buying fleece for years need to do lots of sampling, swatching, and experimenting to see which combinations of preparation and spinning technique bring out the best in the fiber, as well as give us the best yarn for the project we have in mind. These three habits will improve your spinning and help you make better decisions about wools you have not yet worked with.

First Considerations

When you see a fleece that might work for the project you have in mind, you should first find out if the fleece is sound. By that I mean, will it hold up to the processing you're going to put it through? Some qualities, such as whether it's brittle or has weak spots, can interfere with good prep. Here are some tests you can use to discover potential problems.

- **Brittle or weak fibers.** Listen to a lock or two, and it may tell you a few things about a fresh fleece. Take one lock about the thickness of your pinky from the fleece and hold it at each end. Bringing it up next to your ear, quickly pull the ends away from each other. A high-pitched ping in a fresh fleece means that the fleece is sound and good. Take another lock and see if it happens again. If the lock breaks or makes a noise like a thud, this could be a sign of a break in it (see below). A crackling sound just might mean it's a brittle fleece that would break easily during carding. This isn't a deal breaker, but it is something to think about. It could be a sign of weakness, because if the fleece isn't fresh (more than three to four months since shearing), you may not expect to get that high-pitched ping. And there could be a bit of crackling that has nothing to do with weakness.

- **Breaks in the fibers.** Hold a few locks up to the light. Can you see a line of finer fiber running horizontally through the locks? This is a weak spot, called a *break*. If an animal has experienced significant stress — through sickness, a drop in nutrition while carrying or raising a lamb, a change in climate, or exposure to severe weather — it can cause a break in the fleece. This weak spot causes the fibers to break easily during processing. If it's in the middle of the lock, I generally pass that fleece by. If it's closer to the tips and I feel like I can do without that bit of length, and if the fleece as a whole is good and clean, then I may buy the fleece with plans to just break the tips off before spinning.

- **Tender tips.** When I look at the lock tips, I pull gently to see if they come off. This is not a bad thing, just something to look at. The tips of the wool are out in the weather all the time and may become a bit brittle or tender. If you comb or flick the locks,

break in fibers

many times the tips just naturally come off. Tender tips can either be cut or pulled off if you plan on carding the fleece. It's important to do this before you begin to card, because they will cause noils if they are allowed to come off during the carding process.

Assessing Lock Length

In the best-case scenario, you've done your homework about the breed (or the breeds in the background, if you're looking at a cross) and know what to expect when you look at the wool. For example, does the fleece you are interested in have attributes that fall within the ranges stated for the breed standard? If you plan to comb or flick this wool, are the locks long enough? If you plan to card or flick this wool, are the locks too long? If you have the fleece right in front of you, it is much easier to make personal judgments, and the breed standard may become a bit less important to your buying decision. (For advice about choosing tools, see Your Choice Matters, page 16.)

I once got so excited about some Lincoln lamb fleeces I had heard were available in another state that I bought them all without ever asking about lock length. Well, I was stuck with 50 pounds of 3- to 4-inch Lincoln. It was too short to comb, and the fibers fell apart when it was carded. The twist I needed to add to keep the yarn together was so high that the resulting yarn was very coarse and wiry. (A shorter staple length means that more twist

is necessary to hold the fibers together in the yarn.) That was one of my first lessons about asking all the right questions. The price was too good to be true, and I learned why.

Shorter-locked wools, such as Southdown, are wonderful to card with handcards or a drumcarder, even if the lock length is only 2 or 3 inches. Don't let a shorter length stop you if that is the breed average. A Southdown is not one I would comb, and I would avoid the flick, because I would surely be hurting my knuckles trying to flick such short locks. So again, end use is something to think about, as the shorter length limits you somewhat in the processing techniques that have an effect on the end-result yarn.

Touch and Feel

The feel of the wool can be misleading when you're faced with choosing an unscoured fleece. The grease in the wool can make it feel softer or harsher than it might be after it is scoured. Once you've chosen many fleeces of the same breed, it's easier to make comparisons by touching several fleeces side by side. A fleece barn at a festival may be a great place to compare a range of wools from the same breed; however, the rush and excitement of the place can cause some buyers to get carried away, and being nervous about the possibility of a lost opportunity may cause "accidental" purchases. Keep calm and remember that the sheep are growing more wool. If you miss one fleece, chances are there is another one right around the corner.

Keep the basic characteristics you know about fleeces in mind as you shop (see page 2). Short, blocky locks with well-formed crimp usually mean the fleece is from a fine-wool breed. Longer, pointy locks with wave or purl rather than crimp are usually longwools. Down and Down-type fleeces are usually harder to find at a fleece sale. Similar to the fine wools, these also have short blocky locks, but the crimp is either difficult to see or broader than what you see in fine wools. Search out these fleeces and use them to help you distinguish how fleeces at each end of the spectrum feel, and go from there. The longwools have a silky feel, for instance, even if the fibers may not be as fine as some others, such as a strong Lincoln.

Digging Deeper

Looking at a few locks can give you an overview of the fleece, but there could be surprises in that bag, so now we're going to go a bit deeper. Here's an overview of what I look for when purchasing fleece.

The fleece roll. A fleece is usually rolled so the cut ends are out. The tips are all inside the roll and hard to see, unless you find where the fleece is rolled together and can look into the middle of the bag. If you see a fleece neatly rolled, it's not a good idea to just begin rooting around. The fleece structure has been maintained in the bag so that when the spinner takes it home, he or she can unroll the fleece and do any sorting desired or necessary. It's pretty important, therefore, to try not to disturb the way the fleece has been arranged in the bag. That said, there are lots of things we want to see that may not be evident by just opening the bag and looking into it.

Skirting. Smart fleece sellers put any tags (by tags, I mean poop) or parts of the fleece that weren't well skirted toward the bottom of the bag. It's important to determine if this is the case with the fleece you're looking at. Let's be frank: fleece will come with some bits of undesired stuff. Don't walk away because somebody missed a small spot. But you do want to avoid big pieces of waste and large areas of wool that may not be usable. Most of the time this is not a huge issue in fleece barns at festivals, but some fleeces available at farms may not have been skirted well. Sometimes this is because the shepherd doesn't think the wool is worth this extra step.

If there is room and time, ask if you can take the fleece out of the bag and open it up. Take this opportunity to tell the shepherd how spinnable the fleece is and how just a three-minute skirting process makes this fleece even more valuable to the spinner. (For information about how to do your own skirting and a photo of an unrolled fleece, see page 10.)

Coated fleeces. Some shepherds coat their sheep to keep the amount of VM to a minimum. A coat is made from strong, tear-resistant fabric and covers the sheep from her neck to the britch (the thigh and rear end of the sheep). It does not go all the way around to cover the belly, so the wool not covered by the coat is removed after shearing when the fleece is skirted. The idea that a coated fleece has less VM to deal with can be enticing. The fact that a fleece has been coated can add several dollars per pound to the price, however, because a lot more time and expense has been invested in the wool. The coats need to be changed regularly either for fresh coats because the sheep got somewhere she shouldn't have and tore it, or because the wool has grown and, therefore, the coat doesn't fit anymore. Some shepherds are experts at coating their sheep and some may not be as skilled. When considering a coated fleece, check the tips of the locks and make sure they aren't felted or tender (easily broken) and that they can be easily separated. Felted or tender tips may be the result of a coat that wasn't changed frequently enough to keep up with the wool growth, so that the coat became too tight, causing abrasion that actually felted the fleece.

Second cuts happen when the shearer runs the clippers down the sheep and then comes back again and re-shears a spot he's already taken wool from. Some little short bits come off with this next run of the shears. A skilled shearer will have very few second cuts. Again, this is not necessarily a reason to walk away from a fleece, unless there is a huge amount. And *my* huge amount may be different from what *you* consider a huge amount. Remove as many of these second cuts as possible before processing the fleece. If you don't, they will add neps and noils to your carded rolags, and thus some possibly unwanted "texture" to your yarn.

Shepherds sometimes protect their sheep's fleece from vegetable matter and other undesirable material by coating them.

Yolk is the combination of secretions from the sheep's skin. It includes sweat, or *suint,* combined with grease or lanolin. The yolk is generally yellow, and it will wash out with scouring. Do not confuse it with stains (see below), which cannot be removed in scouring. The difference between the two, however, may be difficult to tell in an unscoured lock.

Canary stain. This yellow stain can appear as either a narrow band or cover a wide part of the tip, and it will not wash out. It happens when the sheep are living in an area where the weather is hot. It seems that the combination of the hot weather and the sheep's sweat causes this stain. Blending fibers helps distribute the color evenly through the yarn, but if it is severe, overdyeing is your best bet to cover up this coloring. When you're buying a fleece, this stain may not be obvious, unless you can wash a lock before making a decision. Depending on how badly you want to use the fleece in its natural color rather than dye it, you may want to avoid canary-stained fleeces, although the discoloration generally does not affect the soundness of the fleece.

Other stains. It's good to make sure there aren't other stains that may not wash out. Green-, blue-, or peach-colored stains are the result of bacteria, but you can usually remove these areas during sorting. If there's a strong yeast smell associated with the wool, it's best not to purchase that particular fleece, as the cause of these kinds of stains may have also affected the strength of the wool.

FLEECE PROBLEMS

second cut

yolk (before and after washing)

canary stain

FLEECE PROBLEMS

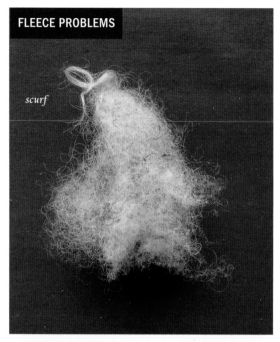

scurf

cotted wool

Scurf is basically skin flakes — an oily dandruff! Some fleeces may have a very tiny bit, and you may not even notice it. If there's enough for you to notice, however, I say walk away from that fleece. Scurf is almost impossible to get rid of. These tiny flakes want to remain glued to the fiber. Although you may be able to remove some if you comb the wool, you won't get it all out, and I'm unaware of chemical processes available at home that will do the job. If it's in your fleece, then it will be in your yarn.

Cotted wool is wool that seems to be glued together or felted in one spot. Most of the cotted wool I have encountered has been in the longwools and the multicoated breeds. Sometimes the cotting appears at the cut end and sometimes mid-lock. One of the causes of cotted wool is a lack of sufficient grease being produced as the fleece grows to keep the fibers from matting. This lack of grease could be because of some illness or lack of a nutrient in the sheep, or because weather conditions (such as long, wet springs) weren't favorable that year. Check more than one place in the fleece; that particular sheep may have liked to rub herself in a certain spot on a certain fence post, and the majority of the fleece may be unaffected.

Cotting can also occur in breeds that naturally shed. If they aren't sheared before the wool begins to lift, the new wool will begin to grow in through the lifted wool, and the two coats may become welded together like a welcome mat.

Some cotting is light enough that the locks can be pulled apart with your hands, and if the price is right, it may be worth trying to process the fleece. If you find that the locks won't pull apart with very little effort, then it is best just to leave the fleece, even if it has the most beautiful long locks you've ever seen. I'm speaking from experience!

Musicality. Once again, give a few locks the test for brittle or weak fibers described under First Considerations on page 27.

Moths and Carpet Beetles

Both clothes moths and carpet beetles love protein fibers, so wool is a big attraction.

Carpet Beetles

The larvae of the carpet beetle are what eat your textile, as well as your wool carpets, furs, leather-bound books, and the fur of dead animals — such as mice that may have died in the walls of your house. Pet hair is also an attraction for them. They usually feed just on the nap, rather than making holes in the base of a carpet, but their irregular eating pattern causes quite a bit of damage nevertheless. Although I've never seen a live carpet beetle, I've noticed the cast-off shells of the larvae around the edges of rooms. The mature beetles fly in from outdoors and lay their eggs on a food source. The eggs are so small that they usually cannot be seen. The way to get rid of these pests is to clean your carpets and the edges of your rooms regularly.

Two types of these beetles are the most worrisome: the varied carpet beetle and the furniture carpet beetle. Both are round and somewhat mottled in their coloring, possibly resembling a ladybug in shape. They can come in on cut flowers or through cracks in windows and doors. The adults are attracted to light, and so you often see them near windows and on windowsills. The larval stage of these bugs is anywhere from 70 to 630 days! And during the larval stage, they are eating your stuff.

To save your fleeces and processed fibers from these annoying things, don't store fleeces on the floor. Either a shelf above the floor or any sealed container is usually enough protection.

If you find them in your stash, you can kill the beetles by exposing them to temperature extremes: Put the fiber in any kind of container, such as a plastic zipper bag, and then into the freezer for two weeks at 18°F (–7.7°C) or less. Alternatively, you can heat the fiber to over 120°F (48.8°C) for at least 30 minutes; aluminum foil is a great container for wool you might want to bake in the oven. In summer, a

carpet beetle larva   *adult carpet beetle*

favorite trick is to put the fiber in a black trash bag and leave the bag in the car, which serves as an oven. If there are many beetles or the damage is great, however, it is best to just discard the fiber.

Moths

I addressed carpet beetles first, because they seem to be the less scary pest for spinners. But now we'll deal with the *M* word and how to protect yourself, or deal with them, if you happen to find them in your beloved wool.

Like carpet beetles, clothes moths live outside around birds' nests and spiderwebs. They come in just like every other insect — with us and on the breeze. These moths, unlike carpet beetles, are not attracted to light. They are more prone to walking than flying and are very small as adults — about ½ inch. They are shiny beige in color, with a darker stripe on their wings. The adult moths mate and lay eggs, which hatch tiny worms (larvae) that immediately begin to eat the protein fibers they are

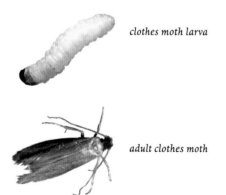

clothes moth larva

adult clothes moth

living on. As with the carpet beetles' larvae, it's the clothes moth's larvae that eat our stuff.

Strategy #1: Prevention. The first line of attack is prevention. I like to put all new fibers in quarantine for about two weeks before I join them with my stash. I'm not saying I always do this, but I know it's the wise thing to do. Quarantined fibers live in the garage or another area away from my clothing, yarns, and fibers.

Strategy #2: Traps. The next line of defense is pheromone traps. These traps contain a little tube of sticky stuff that attracts the male moths, who enter the tube to check it out and get stuck on it. Don't worry, people can't smell it. You want to capture the males so they aren't available for breeding. Equally important, if you have these traps and check them regularly, you'll be alerted to whether moths are present before the situation gets way out of control. When purchasing these (available at hardware stores and from your exterminator), make sure to look for traps specifically formulated for clothes moths. Traps are available for pantry moths, too, but these traps contain a different pheromone, which does not attract the male clothes moth.

Strategy #3: Light. These moths do not like light. They like small, enclosed, still, dark spaces, so closets are their favorite hideouts. Dig into your stash a lot. Move things around. Air it out.

Strategy #4: Heat. A good bake in a hot car in the summer can do wonders! Put your fibers in black plastic bags and fill your car with them on a very hot day. Heating for several hours at temperatures over 120°F (48.8°C) kills adults, eggs, and larvae. My car and yours are perfect for this job in hot weather. Since there are generally two generations a year if the moths are allowed to propagate, this car oven will stop an infestation in its tracks.

Strategy #5: Freeze. Freezing can work, but it's a lot more work than the cooking-in-the-car method. Freezing kills only the live moths and larvae; it does nothing to the eggs, which means you have to follow a timed process for this to work. Put the suspected item in a container such as a plastic bag or other sealed receptacle, and place the container in the freezer for several days, then take it out and wait for about two weeks. The eggs hatch in 4 to 10 days, so if there are any eggs, they will hatch within two weeks. After that time, return the item to the freezer for several days.

Strategy #6: Dry-ice fumigation. Put the suspect items in an airtight container or thick plastic bag along with dry ice. One-half to one pound of dry ice to a 30-gallon container is usually enough. Close the bag or the container loosely, so air can escape as the dry ice vaporizes; sealing the bag tightly may cause it to pop due to increasing pressure. When the dry ice is gone, tightly seal the container or bag and let it sit for three or four days. This will kill all stages of the moth.

If you do all of these things and still end up with moths in a part of your stash, do not panic. So that uncontaminated items aren't infested, I generally do not try to save infested items. Whenever I see evidence of moths or larvae, I just remove the items and discard them. The larvae often have done enough damage to the fiber and yarn that it's difficult to use even if I try to work with it.

My intention here is not to instill fear for the safety of your wool. Clothes moths are a part of nature and so a fact of life, especially for those of us who love protein fibers. I hope that, by using these strategies, nothing will get out of control, and the place where the moths entered your stash will also be their exit with as little lost wool as possible.

Chapter 3

GETTING TO
YARN

SPINNING IS NOT AN END IN ITSELF: It's a way to get yarn to make other things. Those spun fibers are used for a huge variety of things in our lives. Many of us don't even notice the textiles that serve us every day. Thread and string and yarn and rope — not to mention the fabrics that are made from them — are all around us. The fibers that make up all of these things have been prepared differently and received different amounts of twist in the spinning in order to make them function well for us.

To discuss the multitude of different fiber preparations and spinning techniques would take a whole book in itself, and so I have chosen here to focus on the uses that I think most handspinners have in mind for their yarns. Yarns for crochet are generally the same as those used in knitting; weaving yarns are a bit different, but not hugely. After learning about these yarns, you may decide you want to create yarns or threads for tatting, or for cross-stitch, crewel, or other embroidery techniques. All of these are very achievable using the techniques that are covered in the following chapters.

Handspun yarns often seem to change like chameleons as they move through the various stages of processing. An unspun fiber that feels nice to the touch can feel a bit crisp or firm as freshly spun yarn. After washing, that same yarn may change a little more, and finally the knit or woven fabric may drape beautifully and again feel soft. As yarn buyers, we fall into the trap of buying yarns based on how soft they are. This doesn't necessarily benefit the end product we have in mind, but those soft balls of Merino call to us. Handspun yarn may not feel like those mill-spun yarns on the shelves, but that's because we're spinning for a purpose. The mill's purpose is to produce a beautiful ball or skein of yarn; our purpose is to go beyond that yarn to the end result we are looking for.

Spinning Yarns for Knitting or Crochet

You'll find both knit and woven samples in this book. I have chosen to use the yarns in these ways because that is what I know best, but this doesn't mean that the yarns aren't good for crochet or bobbin lace or other types of needlework. Make your samples using the techniques and skills that you have. Handspun yarn can work in any project that calls for yarn.

How to Spin for Smooth Knitting

By smooth knitting, I mean fabric that has no stitch patterning, such as cables or textural stitches. Yarn for smooth knitting doesn't necessarily need to be smooth yarn, and, in fact, this is where fuzzy woolen yarns come in very handy. It's also where those bouclés you love can be used. In other words, it's where you can feature the yarns rather than the stitch patterns. The yarn in the photo below is woolen spun and 3-ply. The halo created in some yarns by the woolen spinning technique is beautiful in a stockinette sweater.

I, personally, usually like a medium twist in the yarn I use for knitting projects. By medium, I mean the twist angle is between 30 and 40 degrees. This twist gives the yarn strength combined with softness. (Other spinners I know like to keep the twist angle in their plied yarns closer to 45 degrees.) Notice I say I *usually* like it for knitting projects. Although

Yarn spun worsted from flicked locks is smooth and when knit up, results in pleasing stitch definition.

that may not give you the solid answer you're looking for, here's a secret: In spinning, there are very few times that one answer is going to work. For example, if I'm spinning a soft fiber, such as Merino or Shetland, I can go for that middle-of-the-road twist. The fiber won't start feeling crisp until I get more than a 50-degree twist angle. (By crisp, I mean firm, not wiry, but no longer soft to the touch.) On the other hand, if I'm spinning something like Lincoln for a cardigan, I want to be down to less than 30 degrees for my twist angle, because Lincoln starts to feel harsh with more than 45 degrees in the twist angle. (The higher the number in the twist angle, the more twists per inch.) Too many numbers? Then don't think about the numbers. Make a few samples, knit them up, and see which fabric you like. (For more advice on twist, see page 44.)

Spinning for Colorwork and Cables

I prefer the yarns I use for colorwork or cables to be smoothly spun, so the colors are crisply defined and the cables and stitch patterns pop up and sit right on top of the knitting. Although this is surely a question of personal taste, for me, these yarns should be 3-ply or more, so that the yarn fills in all the spaces. These are also the yarns I prefer to spin worsted to make sure I get the most pop from the knitting.

Combed locks spun worsted are ideal for a knit fabric in which cables are the focal point.

Both of these lace samples were spun with the same drafting technique and knit using the same stitch pattern. The major difference between them is their wool type: (LEFT) *Lincoln, a longwool;* (RIGHT) *Suffolk, a Down type.*

Spinning for Lace

Lace yarns are generally thought of as finely spun, and that's where the description ends. The lace yarns I spun for samples in this book are all 2-ply with medium- to low-ply twist, depending on the wool being used. I've spun them based on a few generalizations, but please remember my ever-repeated refrain (which I will continue to repeat until my grave): sample and swatch!

A 2-ply yarn for lace is good because when it's knit, the two sides of the stitch seem to push away from each other, allowing the holes in the lace to be open and cleaner cut. Yarns with more than two plies can be used for lace, but they may not give as good an end result as just two plies.

When you ply your lace knitting yarn, take into account what kind of fabric you are going for. More twist gives a firmer yarn, which in turn gives a firmer fabric. Less twist gives a yarn with more drape and, therefore, a fabric with more drape. Consider whether you're looking for a lace sweater with some body, or a lace shawl that you can wrap close to you and that moves beautifully with you. You should also consider needle size and gauge, of course, but planning the amount of twist, in both your singles and your plied yarn, is the first step toward getting the lace you want.

A Word about Singles and Lace

Twist is an amazing thing: it adds strength to the yarn you are making. Even though the lace samples shown in this book were all knit with 2-ply yarns, you can knit perfectly good lace with singles. As long as the yarn is sound to begin with, the interlacement makes a strong fabric when it's knit, and there is no worry about the yarn breaking during blocking.

Biasing happens when there's excess twist in only one direction. You don't have to worry about biasing in a lace fabric knit with singles yarn, because the piece will be blocked and dry in the position you want it to stay in. The key is to make a sound singles, which means that it needs enough twist to hold together. Here are two things to keep in mind to avoid biasing.

- Flat pieces knit with singles yarn will be more successful than three-dimensional ones, because it's easier to block flat pieces well. If you are making a three-dimensional lace piece, such as a cardigan, it's preferable to use a 2-ply yarn, as these items are more difficult to block and avoid the biasing.

- More biasing happens with more twist, and in order to spin shorter-stapled fibers fine, you need to give them more twist. So, if you really want to a low-twist singles without having to worry about bias in your final project, choosing a wool with a longer-staple length will help. Remember that in a lace project that will be blocked with pins or wires, this is not such a worry.

Spinning Yarns for Weaving

The myth about handspun yarns is that they aren't strong enough for warp, and so the best thing to do is buy your warp and use handspun for weft. Yes, that's a myth. Handspun yarns were used in weaving for thousands of years before a spinning mill was even dreamed of. The secret is to adjust your loom tension and weaving technique to match your yarn, and look for the following characteristics in the yarn: It has to hold together, which means it needs twist, and it should be somewhat smooth. A smooth yarn is desirable because it must be able to easily advance through any slots or holes in the reed or heddles, as well as withstand the abrasion and rubbing from the reed and heddles it receives when beaten many times before being advanced. This is true for any loom with heddles or a reed that the yarn has to go through. A weft yarn doesn't need to stand up to so much tension and abrasion, and so it may be spun differently than the yarns we might use for warp.

All but one of the samples shown in this book are woven with 2-ply yarn, but don't let that stop you from moving in all directions. You can weave beautiful cloth with singles, 2-ply, 3-ply, and more. Changing the number of plies changes the hand, which, simply said, is how the fabric feels. The drape of the fabric also changes with the number of plies. Change the amount of twist in the yarn, and you have a different fabric again. Change the weave structure from plain weave to twill to huck lace to overshot, and the whole thing is different again. When I think about the possibilities, it makes me want to start sampling!

How Much Twist for Warp Yarns?

Lots of twist is sometimes a necessity. You want lots of twist if the warp is going to have to stand up to a lot of tension for some reason, such as warp for a backstrap loom or for a high-tension loom used in Navajo weaving. A floor loom or rigid-heddle loom can use a bit less tension if a lower-twist yarn is needed for the project. Keep in mind that the tension of the loom is spread evenly over the number of threads in the warp. A yarn that may break very easily, therefore, if it is the only strand under tension, may stand up well to the same amount of tension if it has lots of neighboring threads to help bear the load. Higher twist also helps the yarn to be more resistant to abrasion in the heddle and reed, because more twist tucks in more fiber ends to make a smoother yarn, which then slides more easily through the loom parts. In addition, a smoother yarn tends not to stick to its neighbors on the loom, which makes changing sheds much easier.

Worsted versus Woolen Warp Yarns

In addition to the value of using a yarn with a high twist for warp, choosing a worsted-spun yarn is also advantageous, because these yarns are compact and usually smooth, again increasing their resistance to abrasion and making

them less likely to stick to their neighbors when you beat and advance the warp. The less the yarns stick together, the less wear there is on the threads. If you use a soft, woolen-spun yarn for your warp, you may need to use a bit less tension and to advance the warp more often to help your yarn stand up to this abrasion. This is because woolen-spun yarns are airier and usually fuzzier than their worsted friends.

A Note on My Woven Samples

The loom I used for my woven samples was a Hokett loom, regular size (7 by 7¾ inches). These small looms are useful for sampling or small tapestries. Little slits cut into the wood at the top and bottom keep the warp yarn aligned and provide a sett of about 8 ends per inch. (*Sett* describes the number of warp threads in each inch of the fabric width.) Most of the yarns I used for these samples should be sett a bit closer for plain weave, but I could get an idea of how the fabric would look without losing a lot of yarn to waste.

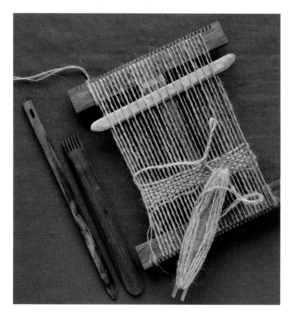

Simple Adjustments for More PLEASURABLE SPINNING

As I teach people to spin, whether they're beginners or more experienced, the adjustment that makes them, their tools, and their hands happier is to reduce tension. Whether using a spinning wheel or a spindle, the place to begin reducing tension is in your hands.

Relax your hands. Holding onto the fiber like it's trying to escape from your hands causes three problems. First, your hands tire very quickly, with the result that you may get cramps and end up not spinning. Open your hands a bit. Spread them apart a little. Try to think of the way you hold the fiber as supporting it, rather than grasping it. The second problem caused by holding on too tight is that the fibers feel like they don't want to move past each other. Opening your hand that supports the fiber supply just a tiny bit allows

Opening and relaxing your hands as you spin results in a more consistent yarn.

those fibers to slide by and into your yarn. Third, you get uneven yarn. This is because when we struggle to draft out that next bit of fiber, we usually pull the fibers too far, causing a thin spot in the yarn. When you're doing a worsted drafting method such as short forward draw and move your pinching hand back again and pull hard, another thin spot develops. If you open that back hand a little, however, things will move easily, and you can get those shorter drafts that result in more consistent yarns.

Reduce wheel tension. Many spinners struggle to hold the yarn back from being pulled into the orifice because they need more time to do what needs to be done. Remember, you are the boss of your wheel. Loosen the wheel's tension, and you can decide when the yarn goes through the orifice. Adjust the tension (known as *take-up*) on your wheel by turning the knobs and trying things out to see how it feels. This is your tool, so learn to use it to its full potential.

When I start spinning, I almost always begin with no take-up. Then, I adjust upward to where the yarn winds on if I allow it, the yarn is taut between my hands and the orifice, but there's no pulling. I use more tension for long draw than for short forward draw, to avoid the little pigtails that develop on the bobbin if I try to force the yarn on too quickly before it's ready to take up.

That's it. Light hands and light take-up tension, and your spinning life will feel much more relaxed. Not to mention that it's much easier on your expensive equipment.

Spinning Singles

I prepared the fibers for spinning the yarns featured in chapter 4 through 8 in a way that I think works well for each fleece category. That doesn't mean that you have to do it exactly the same way. For example, I processed all the Cormo skeins in the fine-wools section with a flick carder. I've also had great success combing Cormo, as long as I kept the passes to a minimum. The yarns I produced from combing were lovely. Cormo that I've carded, on the other hand, has been more of a learning experience and tends to get neppy more quickly. Slow and full movements are key, as well as a lot of practice and trial and error. In other words, come to this with an open mind and use my directions as a guide and starting point, but don't be afraid to try new things and see what happens.

Choosing the Right Drafting Method

After the wool is processed comes the task of choosing a drafting method that gives you the yarn you want. Drafting methods that keep the twist out of the fiber supply and smooth the fibers at the same time give more of a worsted yarn, even when combined with a preparation method that isn't considered a worsted prep, such as carding. Drafting methods that allow twist and air into the fiber supply give a more woolen end result, even when combined with a preparation method considered to be a worsted method, such as combing. Decide how you're going to use your yarn and whether you want it to have a smooth, crisp look, or

warmth and a "squoosh" factor. Try different drafting methods, and then knit the yarns into small swatches to see what results you get. (For photos of worsted and woolen methods, see pages 14–15.)

Getting Twist Right

In addition to deciding which drafting method to use, you need to consider how much twist to add to your yarn. One way to decide is by looking at the crimp in the wool fibers. Although it's not always the case, closer, tighter crimp (that is more crimps per inch) may mean a finer wool. In addition, a tighter crimp often coincides with a short staple length. When you're evaluating a fleece and trying to decide how to handle it, these characteristics are good indicators that you're dealing with a fine-wool breed. You can use these clues to help you decide the best way to spin the wool you have and the best uses for it.

I learned this when I first started spinning and had no inkling how important spinning would become in my life. Anne Field's *Spinning Wool: Beyond the Basics* was my guide. I read this book, and took her basics and ran with them. She presents the idea of spinning so that the twists per inch in the yarn match the crimps per inch in the fiber. That is the basic approach I have taken in the experimentation with breed-specific wools that I have done for this book. It is a way to begin thinking about, and making, yarns. Crimp is something we can evaluate with very simple tools, and it can give us clues about ways to start using this delicious fiber that we all seem to collect so easily.

As Anne Field herself notes, however, it is important to remember that spinning with crimp in mind is a starting place, and when you plan an actual project (rather than a study) it is important to focus on the requirements of that final goal. Some projects will call for more twist than this formula suggests, and others will call for less.

But when you are learning about wool, it is good to have guidelines. Here are some generalizations you can make, based on the crimp you see. Keep in mind that the generalizations are only that, and each individual situation is different.

- In general, the finer the wool, the more crimps per inch.

- In general, the stronger (or more coarse) the wool, the longer the staple length.

- In general, the stronger the wool, the more the crimp can resemble curly or wavy hair.

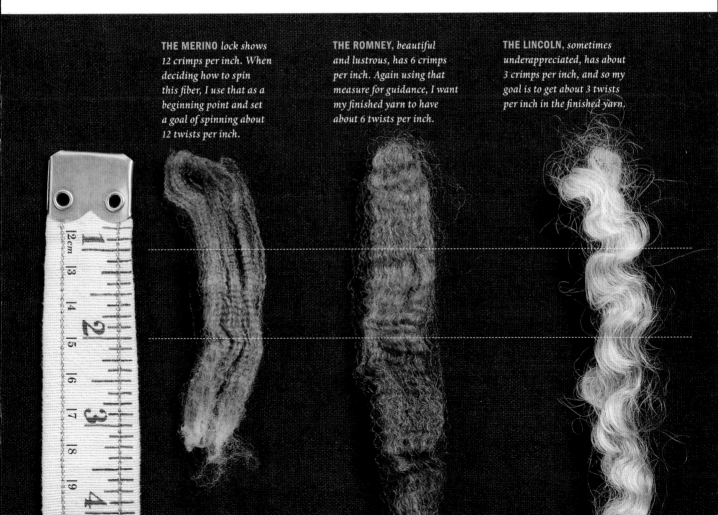

THE MERINO *lock shows 12 crimps per inch. When deciding how to spin this fiber, I use that as a beginning point and set a goal of spinning about 12 twists per inch.*

THE ROMNEY, *beautiful and lustrous, has 6 crimps per inch. Again using that measure for guidance, I want my finished yarn to have about 6 twists per inch.*

THE LINCOLN, *sometimes underappreciated, has about 3 crimps per inch, and so my goal is to get about 3 twists per inch in the finished yarn.*

Often, we make the decision to spin a fine yarn when we're working with a fine wool (not necessarily gossamer). Similarly, with a coarse or strong wool, we spin a thicker yarn, though not necessarily a bulky weight. We take a clue from the way the wool looks to decide what kind of yarn to spin with it.

Let's consider three different kinds of wool: Merino, because it's seen as a standard of fine wool throughout the world; Romney, because it's a good mid-range wool; and Lincoln, because it's much less fine than Merino. In the photos of unwashed locks of these three breeds on the previous page, notice the differences in the crimp of each.

I spin a lot on my Schacht Matchless wheel. The high-speed whorl on my Matchless gives me a high-end ratio of 19:1, and the super-high-speed whorl gives me a ratio of 22:1. I choose a ratio that's close to the twists per inch that I want: for the Merino, the 19:1 ratio. The wheel goes around one turn each time you treadle, and each time the wheel goes around, the flyer turns 19 times. (If you have a double treadle wheel, count on only one foot.)

Adjusting for Different Whorls

If you don't have a high-speed whorl and can spin only at a ratio of 11:1, treadle twice for each draft. (Double-treadle people: remember to focus on only one foot.) We're using a tiny bit of math here, but once you get the idea, this will become natural, and the calculations won't be needed so much.

Note that if you treadle twice each time you draft 1 inch with a wheel at an 11:1 ratio, you get about 22 twists per inch, whereas the goal for the Merino yarn shown on page 45 is 19. You can fix this by drafting a bit more than an inch, but you don't really have to worry about being so precise in the calculations. Your main concern is to spin all the fiber for the project the same way. When this singles yarn spun at 22 twists per inch is plied, the finished yarn will have about 14 twists per inch (tpi), whereas the goal is 12 tpi after ply-ing. Not a very huge difference to worry about.

The whorl of a spinning wheel is also referred to by some spinning teachers as a pulley. The drive band goes around both the drive wheel and the whorl, which turns either the bobbin or the flyer, depending on which drive system your wheel uses. The turning of the bobbin or flyer then adds twist to your yarn. Whorls can have two, three, or even more indentations in them where you can put your drive band. These ridges change the number of rotations the flyer or bobbin makes during one full rotation of the drive wheel. This is referred to as the ratio.

In the photo on the facing page, my wheel is set up with the super-high-speed whorl. I focus on counting only the number of times I treadle with my right foot, as that is the one easier for me to think about. Each time my right foot goes down, the wheel turns once, and, in this case, I draft out 1 inch. This works in short forward draw or in long draw. You just have to watch the length of your draft to match the number of rotations or treadles you do. It can feel a little awkward at first if you don't generally spin this way, but after a while you get into a rhythm and no longer have to count.

You can use this approach for other drafting methods, too. You don't have to be boxed in and use short forward draw for all the yarn you spin based on the crimp, but you do need to keep the number of treadles and the length of your draw in mind.

If you are using a long draw and have a goal of 22 twists per inch, draft out about 10 inches to 12 treadles. I know this may sound like a bit of work, but once you get the rhythm down, it is very simple to do, doesn't take a lot of thought, and can become sort of meditative. Note that it is impossible to have a balanced singles yarn. We are going for stability here. A singles yarn that hangs mostly straight when skeined and washed is stable. (For information about balance, see page 53.) To make sure you're on the right track, lay a sample of spun yarn on the angle graph below, and do a ply-back sample at your wheel following the advice in Measuring Angle of Twist on page 48.

After you have the yarn you want and know the twist angle you're shooting for, count the twists per inch and match it to a whorl size that might work better if you want to increase or decrease your spinning or plying speed.

It's a good idea to keep samples of both the singles and the plied-back yarn that you're finally satisfied with. Wrap them around a business or index card, along with notes about what the fiber is; what wheel, whorl, and treadling/drafting speed you used; and whatever other notes are important to you. This card will be a handy reference when it's time to ply your singles. It is also a great tool to help you maintain consistency when you're spinning a large amount of wool. And finally, when your project is finished, you can put this card, along with your gauge swatches, in your spinning journal as reference for future projects.

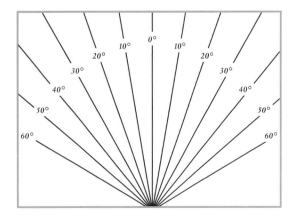

Angle graph

MEASURING ANGLE OF TWIST

To check the angle of twist when you're making 2-ply yarn, take a 24-inch length of your singles and let it fold back on itself to create a 2-ply sample about 12 inches long (a). I have a secret about ply-back samples: They lie to you if you don't use the yarn that is already on the bobbin for this test. Lay this sample on the angle graph and observe where the line of twist in the middle of the sample parallels one of the angle measurements (b). (Use the angle graph shown on page 47 or a protractor for your own sample.)

Without stretching out the yarn, use a ruler to measure the number of twists you're getting (c). If your count is approximately your goal, take that sample and attach it to a card or your wheel to refer to as you spin. If it's a bit off, then change your treadling and drafting accordingly.

If your goal is to get a balanced 2-ply yarn and you are satisfied with your sample, you can calculate the angle of twist you need to put in your singles in order to achieve the twist you want in the 2-ply consistently. When you ply a singles for a balanced 2-ply yarn, it loses about

one-third of its twist angle, so you have to put more twist in the singles to compensate for this. For example, to get about a 45-degree angle in a 2-ply yarn, try to spin your singles to a twist of about 65 degrees.

This all feels a bit complicated, doesn't it? Having this plied-back sample to check, however, helps you focus on your desired end result as you spin. Measuring a plied sample is particularly useful when you're working with a fine or dark-colored singles.

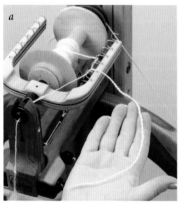

Ply-back sample

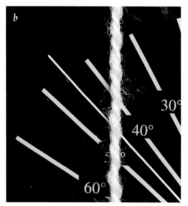

Angle graph

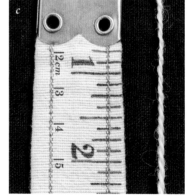

To count the twists per inch in a plied yarn, lay a ruler next to it and count the bumps on one side, then divide by the number of plies. This yarn has 4 twists per inch.

Planning Ahead for Plying

When we set the goals for twist just described, it's helpful to look ahead and have a little understanding of what happens when you ply that yarn. As mentioned earlier, the singles loses some twist while you're plying it, because you're adding twist in the opposite direction. This means that when you spin singles you plan to ply, you need to add a bit more twist than if you were leaving it as singles. If you want to get 12 twists per inch in the plied yarn, for example, you need to add about one-and-a-half times more twist than you would if you were planning to use the yarn as singles, so you should shoot for 18 twists per inch in singles that will be plied. You can accomplish this goal by choosing the appropriate whorl and by adjusting the number of times you treadle each time you draft, just as described on pages 46–47.

Plying Your Singles

Now you've got the hang of spinning the singles, it's time to ply. Hopefully, you saved that little ply-back sample that you made while spinning your singles. Because most of the yarns I spin are smooth and as consistent as possible, that's what I focus on here. If you are interested in exploring more varieties of yarns, you can find great references for how to spin a wide range of textures and artistic-looking yarns, including *The Spinner's Book of Yarn Designs* by Sarah Anderson (see Reading List on page 238).

Getting the Twist Right

Plying can make or break your yarn. It is just as important to the finished product as spinning the singles. On the one hand, too much ply twist and you end up with a very wiry yarn that weaves or knits up into a fabric no one wants to wear and that also may be too brittle to hold up. On the other hand, too little ply twist may result in a yarn that doesn't stand up to any abrasion at all; it may also readily split when you work with it and appear to be two separate strands in the finished fabric. Those are the two extremes, but there's a wide range of great yarns in between.

I take into account several criteria when deciding how much twist to add. My starting point is almost always how much crimp there is in the lock of the raw fleece. This is true even if I'm spinning fibers that have been processed in a large mill and the crimp is not obvious without very close inspection. This is not my only consideration, but it's a convenient place to begin evaluating the fleece and my options.

The next thing I think about is what I want to use the yarn for. Ideally, I thought this through before I spun the singles, but plying is an opportunity to revisit my approach. I usually want more bounce in a sock yarn, so when I work with a very crimpy fiber, such as Polwarth, I spin the singles with twist to match the crimp, and then instead of striving for a completely balanced yarn, I add extra twist — a quarter to a third more — when I ply. This doesn't necessarily work for fibers with less crimp, so that's why it's important to sample.

On the other hand, for a fabric with luster, that drapes and hangs nicely or has a bit of swing, I would have chosen a fiber that might more easily give me these qualities, but then I put a bit less twist in the ply. How much less twist depends on the project I have in mind, including whether it needs to stand up to a lot of wear or will be a shoulder shawl and therefore not subjected to a lot of abrasion.

Choosing the Number of Plies

The amount of plying twist isn't my only consideration. I must also decide how many plies to use, and again, this depends on the project. A 2-ply yarn is great for knitted lace work, because it tends to be flat, which helps keep those holes open. A 3-ply yarn is rounder and therefore tends to close up the open spaces in knitting, making it great for solid fabrics. A 3- or more ply yarn also helps create a more uniform knit fabric. Many people feel that a 2-ply yarn is best for woven fabrics, though I have come to understand that a 3-ply may result in a fabric with more drape, but I haven't yet experimented with this possibility. A 4-ply yarn is round, beautiful, and also more durable. In addition, more plying twist combined with additional plies can help to even out inconsistencies in your yarn.

Using the Yarn

Finally, the way you knit or weave also affects your results. In weaving will you sett the threads close or further apart? What needle or hook size will you knit or crochet with? Again, this is why sampling all the way through to a washed and blocked swatch is so very important.

When You're Using a Handspindle

When you're plying with a spindle, the feeling is all in your hands and in your eyes. As you get a rhythm and learn to feel the speed of the twist as you draft, you'll get an idea of when to add more twist. This all comes with practice. A ply-back sample is just as helpful when using a spindle as when treadling a wheel.

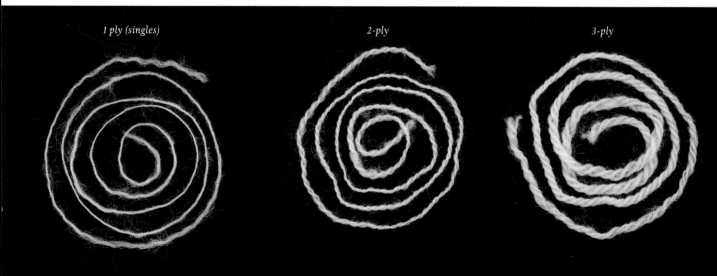

1 ply (singles)   *2-ply*   *3-ply*

Choosing and Using a LAZY KATE

When you buy a spinning wheel, it usually includes a lazy kate, which is designed to hold your bobbins full of singles and allow you to ply two (or more) singles together. The one that comes with your wheel may not be the one that makes you happiest, however, so you may want to hunt for one that works better for you. My favorite lazy kate design is one where the bobbins sit at about a 45-degree angle. This angle provides natural tension so there's usually no need for a tensioning string. If the bobbins sit parallel to the floor in your kate, you'll need to provide some kind of tension to avoid overspinning as you ply. Take care to create only enough tension to help them slow down a bit, not so much that you have to pull hard to get the yarn to come to you, or you'll find your singles breaking at points with a bit less twist. If your kate holds the bobbins upright, you may or may not need tension, depending on the yarn you are plying. It's sometimes difficult to ply very fine yarns when the bobbins are upright, but it depends on the exact design of the kate and the way the bobbins rotate.

In some cases, the lazy kate is actually attached to the wheel, which can be very convenient. I do like an on-board kate when I'm traveling to classes and plying just small amounts of yarn, but for general spinning when I'm plying full bobbins, this is not the best way to go. Consistency is the key to getting even twist over the whole bobbin or skein. A kate that sits in front of you requires the yarn be pulled back toward your body and then change direction to be fed onto the bobbin. In my experience, this causes inconsistencies in the twist and so results in inconsistent yarn, even if the singles is extremely consistent.

My lazy kate feels best when it is placed a few feet behind me directly behind my stationary hand. I use a 5-feet-long leader on my bobbins, so that when I finish plying the bobbin, I don't have to twist around to get that last length of singles to come to me. It comes right to my hand.

Finding a Plying Rhythm

If you are plying on a wheel, you can use the same thinking about ratios, treadling, and drafting you used for spinning singles to get the plied yarn you want. Your goal for the Merino was 12 twists per inch in the finished 2-ply to match the 12 crimps per inch in the raw fiber. Again, you can use the 11:1 ratio, and ply about 1 inch of yarn per treadle. Use whatever plying method you like, but try to develop a rhythm so that you get the desired end result.

Smooth and rhythmic, my favorite plying method feels very circular to me. I hold the strands of yarn in the hand with which I usually hold unspun fiber, and I keep this hand stationary, usually resting on my hip. By keeping it stationary, I maintain a constant point from which to measure each feed of yarn, ensuring

that each is the same length. I like to separate the strands with my fingers (a). This helps me to maintain consistent tension on both threads so that when I add twist, they turn around an invisible center core, rather than having one of the lesser-tensioned strands wrap around one or more strands that are held more tautly.

At the same time, I use my forward hand to control how the twist enters the yarn. Further, to ensure that the twist is consistent throughout the process, I move this hand forward and back the same distance with each feed of the yarn. To do this, I move my forward hand slowly back as I treadle, pinching the yarn just behind the twist and moving in a rhythm dependent on the desired effect (b). For example, if I want 12 twists per inch and I have a whorl that is 12:1 and my hands are about 12 inches apart, I

(a) *The forward hand controls the twist entering the singles, while also controlling the length of each feed onto the bobbin.*

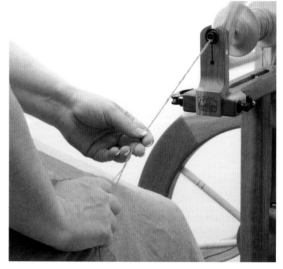

(b) *The back hand remains in place while it controls the singles, so there is even tension on each; it also feels for "pigtails" or ply backs.*

slowly move my forward hand back toward my back hand over the time it takes me to treadle 11 times; on the 12th treadle, I move my hand forward, allowing the newly plied yarn onto the bobbin. I then begin the counting again as I move my hand back from the bobbin to my stationary hand. After a few minutes of counting, the rhythm is set and I no longer need to count, although I occasionally check myself as I ply to make sure I'm still using the same rhythm I began with. This insurance is similar to checking your knitting gauge throughout a project or measuring your picks per inch periodically over the length of yardage you are weaving.

In addition to checking your rhythm, be sure to pull some of the plied yarn from the bobbin every once in a while and lay it next to your sample to make sure you're still on the right track (c).

(c) *As you ply, occasionally stop and compare your yarn with your sample.*

When you do this, don't stretch the yarn; allow it to relax so you can see how it wants to be. Adjust your hands and feet a bit if you're getting too much or too little twist. You may want to add a bit more twist than you have in the ply-back sample, because some of the twist seemingly disappears when you wash and finish the yarn.

Balancing Act

Notice that I didn't refer much to balance in this section on plying. While it's important not to have extreme amounts of twist (too much or too little) in your yarn, some energy won't hurt. In fact, it can sometimes even be beneficial, as in the example of sock yarn on page 49, where that combination of low-twist singles, high-twist ply, and crimpy wool all work together to make a naturally elastic yarn. Like analyzing the fiber crimp, striving for a balanced yarn is just one factor to take into account when you decide how much twist to add. That's the purpose of using the ply-back sample as reference, but it's just a suggestion of what to try for. Remember that you are the boss of your yarn. That's why we spin — to get the yarn we really want in the end.

Perfectly balanced yarn is said to be one with the exact amount of ply twist to offset the twist in the singles so that the finished skein hangs beautifully straight. Perfect balance is not, however, always terribly important. If you plan to enter your skeins in a competition, then make sure that the balance is right on. If the yarn is for your own use, however, you can decide what will make your yarn work best for what you have in mind. If your skein has only one twist after finishing, this will probably not

(LEFT) *This skein has a tight ply (the whole skein has an S twist); it would be excellent for a hard-wearing fabric.* (MIDDLE) *This skein is balanced, and it's the one you could enter in a competition. It would also be great for a wide range of fabrics.* (RIGHT) *This skein, with less ply twist (the whole skein has a Z twist), may work up into a knit fabric with nicer drape than the other two, making it a nice option for a lace project.*

negatively affect your final fabric, although you might see biasing in your fabric if the skein twists more than one or one-and-a-half times. To ensure that you achieve your goal, be sure to make a swatch and block it before committing to an approach.

Many spinners expect their freshly plied yarn to be perfectly balanced right after they remove a skein wound straight from the bobbin. This probably won't occur, however. As you spin your singles and the yarn is wound onto the bobbin, the twist begins to go dormant. Even within a few hours, the yarn won't act the same when plied back on itself as it did when it was completely fresh. Now imagine it has taken a few days or weeks to spin the yarn or that the yarn has been sitting on the bobbin for months waiting for you to get around to plying it. By this time, the twist may be

completely dormant. For this reason, when you remove the yarn from the niddy noddy or skeiner, it will appear to be overspun until you finish it with a nice soak.

Even if you are spinning small samples and ply the samples within minutes, the look of the twist will change when you finish it, no matter how you choose to do so. Even a 15-minute soak in hot water will affect the look of the twist, some of which always seems to dissolve in the soaking water. For over-twisted yarns, an aggressive finish, such as using a plunger or giving it a bit of beating after the soak, may help the skein to hang more straight. If you still think the twist isn't right after finishing, you can run it through your spinning wheel again to add or remove twist. Generally you need just a tiny bit more or less, and so you may want to increase the take-up tension on the wheel, so that you can run it through more quickly. At this point, it is usually in a skein, so instead of winding it onto a bobbin to make this little

Checking Your Balance

If you are going for that perfectly balanced skein and want to check while you're spinning to see if your yarn is balanced, here's a little trick you can use.

Make a ply-back sample and look at the direction the fibers are taking. The fibers that were originally slanted in the singles yarn should now be parallel to the edge of the yarn. If they still slant in the original direction, more ply twist is needed. If they slant in the direction of the plying twist, the yarn has been over-plied.

correction, I just set up my swift nearby and run it onto the wheel straight from there. This doesn't give the precise amount of twist you might originally have planned for, but it can help to correct things. Remember to finish the yarn in water with whatever technique you choose, however, before you decide there's too much twist. Also, if you think there's too little twist and you haven't yet soaked the yarn, you can feel confident that there is in fact too little twist, as you will lose some twist in the finishing.

Finishing Your Yarns

Yarns for knitting, crochet, and needlework should be finished in ways that highlight their beauty, and so no yarn is finished until it is washed. That is when the true nature of your yarn is revealed and you discover what it wants to be. The soak helps even out the twist, and the skein shrinks and the yarn plumps: it's almost like magic. There are two reasons for this. First, because you remove a bit of the singles twist when you ply, there's a little more room for the fibers to move away from each other, as they aren't held in there so snugly. The second cause is that crimp again. Wool has something often referred to as *memory*: crimp wants to stay crimpy. It wants to revert to its original form. While you're spinning it (especially if you use a worsted-type draw), that crimp is getting stretched out, moving those fibers closer to their friends and squeezing the air out. When you wash the finished yarn, it decides there

must be a party going on, and it lets its true self back out. The crimp returns as close as possible to its original shape. This makes the length of the skein shrink and push out a bit to the sides, and it also changes the number of twists per inch in very crimpy fine wools, such as Merino or Cormo. If there are 12 twists per inch before washing, the twists may be closer together afterward. This after-wash change differs depending on the type of wool you have. A wool like Merino tends to bounce back quite a bit because of the amount of crimp in that fiber. The Lincoln, on the other hand, has very little bounce-back or shrinkage. When you spin, you can make allowances for this tendency simply by removing an extra twist or two if you are spinning a really bouncy wool.

The Fulling Process

A process done with fibers that have already been spun into yarn, fulling helps to unify the fibers in the yarn. It also makes some yarns stronger, so that they are more resistant to pilling and can better stand up to abrasion. In addition, fulling softens yarns and makes them feel more luxurious, and it can make some yarns a bit fuzzier or begin to bring out a halo in them.

Fulling versus Felting

Fulling and felting are both done to make fibers stick together, but felting is a different process from fulling and has a very different end result. To felt, unspun fibers are arranged in layers, with each layer usually perpendicular to the one beneath, moistened with soap and water, and then subjected to rubbing until they bond in a cohesive fabric.

Finally, it helps to even out a yarn and make it appear more consistent, especially if the yarn was spun with a woolen method, such as long draw. I don't usually use the finishing methods I describe here for yarns that I have prepared or spun using worsted methods, because I want those yarns to remain a little denser and less fuzzy than yarns I prepare and spin with a woolen method. As with so many things in spinning, it's all about end use.

I have three different methods for fulling yarns. Two of them involve a bucket of hot water and a bucket of cold water.

Method 1, the gentle one. Add an eighth to a quarter teaspoon of detergent or soap to a bucket of hot water. Have a bucket of cold water ready. To open the scales on the wool fibers, place the yarn into the hot water first. Remove the skein from the hot water and immediately plunge it into the cold water. Leave it there for a very short time, then put it back in the hot water. Continue to dunk the skein back and forth between the two buckets three or four times, or just until the strands of yarn begin to stick together. At this point, stop: you don't want the strands to become inseparable.

Method 2. This method is a little more aggressive, and you need a clean, short-handled sink plunger for it. In addition to working with wool, it is great to use on cashmere, bison, yak, and other downy, short-stapled fibers. Follow the same procedure described for Method 1, but when the skein is in the hot water, take a plunger to it. Don't be shy: plunge it a lot,

Finishing using a plunger in one of two buckets

Soap or Detergent?

Soaps are generally more alkaline than detergents. This alkalinity can help to open up the wool scales, so if fulling or felting is your goal, then soap might be a great choice. If you aren't interested in fulling your yarn, choose the less basic pH that detergent will provide. Wool is least likely to full or felt at a pH between 3 and 6 because the scales of the wool close at that range.

Of course, heat and agitation are needed to full and felt wool, but choosing the right additive can help or hinder the process. Regardless of which you use, be sure to rinse thoroughly to bring the wool back to a near-neutral pH.

then move it to the cold water bucket. When it goes back to the hot water, again plunge several times. Continue as for Method 1 until the strands begin to stick together.

Method 3, the violent one. You can choose to give the skein the hot-and-cold-water treatment described for the first two methods, or just give it a hot-water soak before you proceed as follows. Remove the extra water from the skein by wrapping it in a towel and pressing on it. Then, holding one end of the skein, smack it several times on a wall, countertop, or whatever hard surface is available. Give the skein about an eighth of a turn and smack it again. Repeat this until you've gone all the way around the skein.

No matter which method you use (even ones that may be scary the first time you do them), lay your skein flat to dry or hang it over the neck of a hanger, turning it a few times while it is drying. Each of these fulling methods gives a result that is slightly different from the others, but difficult to show in photographs. Again, experiment, and then use the method(s) you love the most.

A Caveat: Finishing Weaving Yarns

Although washing is always necessary after spinning, you may not want to give plied yarns intended for weaving the slight fulling and other finishing treatments you give yarns meant for other purposes. Instead of finishing the yarn before using it, therefore, handweavers often give the woven fabric a bit of fulling in the washing machine and dryer after it comes off the loom. I know this sounds scary, and it made me very nervous the first time I did it! I was lucky to have a very experienced weaver holding my hand throughout the process and reassuring me that all would be okay. And it was. So, generally speaking, save the fulling process until after you've woven the fabric.

There is one other caveat: if you are weaving with singles yarns, you should full the warp a bit using one of the above methods *before* you use it, in order to give it added strength. Even after this slight bit of fulling before the yarn becomes fabric, there will still be enough room between the fibers so they can move while the fabric is being finished, providing that last bit of fulling that makes the fabric cohesive.

Playing with Twist and Size

We can make certain assumptions about the thickness of a yarn we're spinning, depending on how many twists per inch we think it needs. One generalization is that the thicker a yarn, the less twist it needs to hold together. The opposite is also true: the finer a yarn, the more twist it needs to hold together. But we can play with these assumptions a bit if we like. Let's start with the Lincoln yarns. The three yarns at the left in the photo on the next page have been spun to approximately 3 twists per inch to match the 3 crimps per inch the fleece has.

These yarns, spun from fleece of three different breeds, offer a wide variety of opportunity; in each case, I based the number of twists per inch on the number of crimps per inch in their fiber.

THREE LINCOLN *yarns spun with three twists per inch, from left to right: laceweight, medium, bulky.*

TWO MERINO *yarns with the same size singles; greater thickness is achieved by using more plies.*

TWO ROMNEY *2-ply yarns were both combed and spun worsted. The lighter-weight one was dizzed; the heavier-weight one was spun from the comb.*

These yarns go from laceweight to medium weight to bulky, each with the same number of twists per inch. All of the Lincoln skeins are soft and drapey. I expect that the finest one, if used for something that gets a lot of wear, will develop a lot of halo and also may pill, as the ends aren't as tucked as I might like, but because the staple length is more than 6 inches, the fibers will stay tucked in better than if we were spinning at this low twist with a shorter staple length.

If I were to spin a bulky, low-twist yarn with Merino, like the two skeins in the middle (opposite), I know it would pill terribly because the staple length is short, making it easy for individual fibers to work their way out of the bundle of fibers. Giving more twist when you spin shorter-stapled fibers helps them not to pill. In addition, shorter-stapled fibers are generally finer fibers whose crimp asks for more twist. It's kind of nice for them to help us out that way. In the case of short-stapled, fine fibers, if I want a yarn that is soft and bulky yet won't pill, I use more plies to get the thickness I want.

I also spun the Romney fleece (two skeins at the right opposite) to different yarn diameters, again with the twists per inch based on the crimp of the fiber. This allows the typical Romney luster to be revealed and the yarn to be soft enough for garment construction.

When you have a coarser fiber that you would usually want to spin for a garment, it is better to spin with a lower twist and thus avoid the wiry, hard yarns you can get if you don't follow the guidance the crimp provides.

Working with Commercially Processed Fibers

With a little bit of investigating, you can get some clues and come to some conclusions about the best spinning techniques and uses for fibers that have been processed by someone other than you. When I look at commercially processed fibers that I'm not familiar with, or don't even know the contents of, the first thing I do is take just one or two fibers from the top (combed prep) or roving (carded prep), lay them against a contrasting background, and try to analyze the crimp. It's hard to be completely precise, but I try to count how many crimps per inch each fiber has. A measuring magnifier or linen tester, available at hobby stores and online, can help make it possible to see what you're doing.

It's sometimes especially hard to distinguish the crimp in fibers that have been heavily processed and then compressed in a heavy *bump* (a cylinder of coiled fibers prepared for spinning, weighing about 10 kilos, or 22 pounds) and stored under lots of other heavy bumps waiting for your fiber store to buy it. If this is the case, or I'm not sure what I'm seeing, when I get my fiber home, I take a small bit the length of a staple, wet it, then press out the water with a towel, and let it dry. If any crimp is left, it will be evident after this procedure. Some of the more ubiquitous wools may be difficult to completely reconstitute when you're trying to distinguish crimp. Processing techniques in the mills, including lots of carding and combing, as well as the use of chemicals,

may very well cause the crimp to relax so much that it won't ever come back to its original state.

Commercial processing may alter a fiber's natural characteristics in a variety of ways. Many retailers get their wools from a variety of suppliers, each of whom may have different processing techniques. The result may be that your finished yarns have a different hand, even from the same breed. Add to that the fact that fleeces are a changeable thing, dependent on weather, feed, and the environment the sheep have been living in, so the supplier you purchased from last year may have fleeces with a very different feel this year.

If, like me, you just want to be in the ballpark when making your spinning decisions, you can look up the breed information. When you know the specific breed of a fiber, you can make some educated guesses about how to spin it by referring to books such as Deborah Robson and Carol Ekarius's *The Fleece and Fiber Sourcebook*, their *Field Guide to Fleece*, or to breed-society websites, where you can usually find information about fiber length and diameter ranges. These averages are a good starting point when you're spinning mill-processed wools. This range will help you to know about how many crimps per inch of staple length to expect. Wools with a micron count of 23 or less generally have 11 or more crimps per inch. Wools with micron counts of between 23 and 31 usually have between 6 and 10 crimps per inch. If the breed measures higher than 31, you can expect it will have 5 or fewer crimps per inch. Of course, these are generalizations, but since the processed wool you are using is made up of lots and lots of fleeces all blended together, you can feel pretty comfortable with these ranges.

If you are unable to analyze the crimp, you still have staple length and fiber thickness to go by when you decide how to prepare and spin any fiber. I always like to have a starting place, so here are some things I look for and think about first when I'm deciding how much twist to put in a yarn.

- Shorter staple length means that you need more twist to hold the fibers together into a yarn. This rule stands regardless of fiber diameter.

- A coarser, thicker fiber diameter generally means you should add less twist if you're spinning a yarn that will be used for a garment. This is because more twist usually results in a coarser, more wiry-feeling yarn, as well as a firm yarn that doesn't drape well.

- Fibers that are best spun into lower-twist yarns are often from longer-stapled fleeces, and less twist is needed to hold these fibers together.

You may not always want to process your fleece from the very beginning, but you can use many of the methods and discoveries I describe here on that mill-processed and possibly hand-dyed fiber in your stash.

Do-It-Yourself Breeds Study

Throughout this book, I stress over and over the importance of sampling and how it can help you get the best yarn and the best fabrics from your spinning. As you sample and learn about different wools, the need for sampling decreases. I've spun the fleeces of more than 55 breeds of sheep, and the first few times I worked with each breed, it was necessary to do multiple samples to see how that fleece would react to different methods of preparation and spinning. I've spun pounds and pounds and pounds of Wensleydale, however, and so I'm now very familiar with Wensleydale fleece. I no longer need to make multiple samples each time I spin it. I may still spin a small sample of the yarn I'm aiming for, but I have a head start because I know what take-up I like on my wheel and which is my favorite ratio to use. If I spin Wensleydale on a handspindle, I know which spindle I would choose. It's similar to knitting, weaving, and crocheting. If you're about to begin a project using yarn you've often used before, a sample swatch may no longer be necessary. You always need to sample yarns that are new to you, but those comfortable yarns you turn to when you just want to just do your thing and not think . . . that is how I feel about Wensleydale.

I've been conducting my own breeds studies and teaching classes about breed characteristics for several years now, and it is one of the most fun things I do. If you don't have the opportunity to take a class with someone, you can do this at home, following the advice I give in this book as I walk you through the process, from getting your first bit of fleece to creating and keeping good records. Your notebook will serve as a reference for more than just a breed's story. You can also use it to record information such as how twist acts in different wools and how the different ratios on your wheel change the wool you are spinning. You'll have a record of which experiment worked best in the past for the yarn you're currently working with, and it will also be valuable if you later decide to use a similar fleece or fiber for a different project. You can just go back to those notes and re-create the yarns.

Creating Your Notebook

Your notebook can be as simple or elaborate as you like. I like to use card stock that is color-coded by fiber category. This helps me quickly flip to the spot in my notebook that I'm looking for. To make these samples, I usually wash enough fleece so that I have at least an ounce of clean wool in the end. This is enough to do three or more good-size samples when I'm spinning medium-weight yarns. I need less for finer yarns and a little more for thick, airy yarns that I want to spin with a long draw. Each sample gets its own card. I wrap some singles around the card and attach 2-, 3-, and 4-ply samples to it. I attach the card, along with a knitted swatch, to a page in my notebook where I jot down all my notes right next to the card. Here are some things I cover:

- **Source of the fiber.** The sheep breed and its source. If the wool was especially beautiful and clean, you don't have to do a major search when you next want to buy from that source.

- **Prep method** (or the prep of purchased fiber). Combed or carded? From a drum-carded batt or flicked locks?

- **Spinning equipment.** Which wheel did I spin the fiber on? Which whorl did I use? (You can describe the whorl using ratios or just by noting which groove you used.) Double drive, Scotch tension, or Irish tension? If you used a spindle, you can note the maker if you like, but the weight of the spindle is even more important to record.

- **Drafting method and drafting length.** Short forward draw, supported long draw, or something else? What drafting length did I use in relation to my treadling? For a worsted draft, like short forward draw, I might say something like "1-inch draft; one draft per two treadles." With this information, if I want to make that exact yarn again, I don't have to guess what I did to get there.

- **Wraps per inch (wpi).** I note wraps per inch of both the singles and the plied samples before and after I finish the yarn because it will change in the finishing. Wraps per inch refers to how many widths of yarn can fit into 1 inch. This can be measured with a special tool or just using a ruler or a dowel with a 1-inch measurement marked on it. Wrap the yarn snugly but don't stretch it or push the strands together too closely. Each wrap should lay comfortably against the previous one. When measuring yarns that are worsted and thicker, it's a good idea to wrap more than 2 inches so that you get a good enough sample to take into account any inconsistencies.

Measuring Yarn Width

Wraps per inch is to the spinner what gauge is to the knitter. It's a tool and reference, but because of the differences in the hands of one spinner to the next, it may not be able to be exactly replicated by someone else. Some knitting designers now include the wpi of the yarn they use in their designs so that it's possible to spin yarn specifically for that project, if desired.

- **Knitted swatch.** I note the needle size I used and the gauge I got.

All of this sampling and note-taking may seem like a lot in the moment, or you may think you'll definitely remember what you did. The voice of experience says you won't. Do yourself a favor and write everything down.

Pure Breeds versus Blends

Throughout this book I discuss only pure breeds in their singular form, because this is the way that I like to begin thinking about breeds. The best characteristics as well as any weaknesses of each wool show when they aren't blended with fleece from another breed.

Once you have this understanding, you can move beyond this knowledge and begin to explore blends of different wools. In this way you can further highlight certain strengths of a breed, and then blend it with another wool with different strengths, to create a combination that may benefit the project you have in mind even more. For example, if you love the luster of the longwools but desire the bounce and airiness of a finer wool, you could blend a finer Wensleydale fleece or top with a crimpy, long-stapled Corriedale. The possibilities are endless. I love the fact that we handspinners can sample until the end of our days and never be able to learn and see all the potential of the wool breeds we have at our disposal.

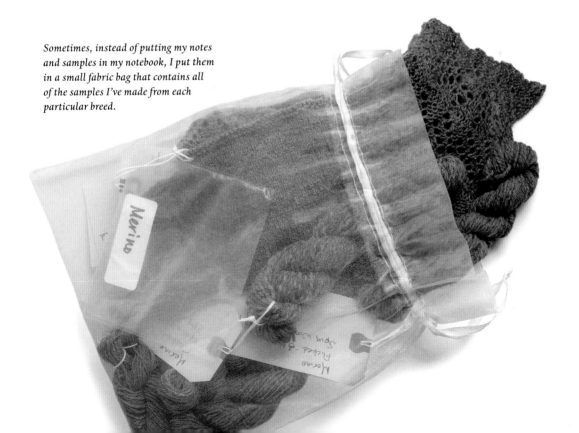

Sometimes, instead of putting my notes and samples in my notebook, I put them in a small fabric bag that contains all of the samples I've made from each particular breed.

Chapter 4

FINE WOOLS

THE FLEECE OF ALL FINE WOOLS is great for making next-to-skin items, anything that needs to be soft. Some wools in the fine wools category are also pretty durable, but due to the shorter staple length of these fibers (usually 5 inches or less), more twist is necessary to avoid pilling, and more twist generally means less soft. So when you're deciding how much twist to add, be sure to take into consideration what use the finished object will have.

The crimp of the fine wools is usually evenly spaced over the length of the lock, and the fine wools generally have a square lock structure, meaning that the tip end is flat. What's great about this is that most of the fibers are the same length. One advantage that most fine wools have is that their fibers are quite dense, and the fleece holds together at the tip, so there are rarely openings to the skin of the animal. This closed fleece helps keep all vegetable matter and other dirt on the outside of the fleece, away from the skin of the animal or the cut end of the lock.

You can easily prepare as well as spin fine wools using either worsted or woolen techniques. This allows you to take advantage of the different properties of these wools. For example, because of their shorter length, these wools work well with a woolen prep, and the fine crimp structure helps make the resulting yarns bouncy and lofty. On the other hand, because of their organized fine crimp, they also lend themselves well to worsted prep and spinning, which adds strength to these more delicate fibers and helps them to resist pilling.

The fine wools tend to be the greasiest of the fleece categories, and they are the most difficult from which to remove the lanolin. Sometimes an additional wash with scour is necessary due to this high grease content. As sheep tend to spend most of their time outside, this extra wax helps maintain the separation of fibers and keeps them from felting right on the sheep.

The following table lists nearly a dozen wools that I classify as fine wools. This chart is by no means all-inclusive, but it gives an idea of the breadth of the category. In addition, the four fine wool breeds I look at in-depth also show how broad this category can be. My descriptions of how I prepped and spun the various fleeces demonstrate how, by making just small changes in any of these processes, you can make a yarn perfect for your project.

Wax, Lanolin, or Grease?

Lanolin is technically a wax rather than a fat or an oil. We spinners use the terms *wax, lanolin,* and *grease* interchangeably to mean the secreted stuff that coats the outside of the fibers.

Characteristics of the FINE WOOLS

Bond

Origin: Merino/Lincoln
Fleece weight: 12–16 lbs.
Staple length: 4"–7"
Fiber diameter: 22–28 microns
Lock characteristics: Dense, blocky, bold crimp
Color: Colored and white

Cormo

Origin: Corriedale/Merino
Fleece weight: 5–12 lbs.
Staple length: 3"–5"
Fiber diameter: 17–23 microns
Lock characteristics: Blocky
Color: Only white can be registered, though a range of browns exist

Corriedale

Origin: Merino/Lincoln
Fleece weight: 12 lbs.
Staple length: 3"–6"
Fiber diameter: 25–35 microns
Lock characteristics: Blocky
Color: White and shades of black and brown

Île-de-France

Origin: Dishley Leicester/Rambouillet
Fleece weight: 6½–10 lbs.
Staple length: 2¾"–3½"
Fiber diameter: 23–30 microns
Lock characteristics: Less blocky tips than usual for fine wools, but dense; regular, fine crimp
Color: White

Merino

Origin: Possibly African rams bred with Spanish ewes in the Middle Ages
Fleece weight: 9–14 lbs. average
Staple length: 2"–5"
Fiber diameter: 11.5–26 microns
Lock characteristics: Blocky tips, dense locks, heavy grease
Color: Usually white, although some blacks and browns are available

Polwarth

Origin: Merino/Lincoln
Fleece weight: 9–13 lbs.
Staple length: 3"–7"
Fiber diameter: 21–26 microns
Lock characteristics: Blocky, with even crimp
Color: Wide range, from whites to blacks to browns

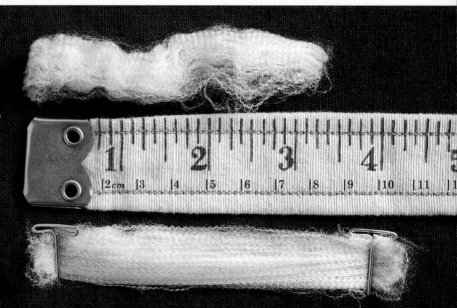

A Word about Staple Length

Staple, or lock, length (top) does not equal fiber length (bottom). To find the full length of the fibers they must be stretched, but lock length is measured without stretching.

Cormo shown here.

Polypay

Origin: Targhee/Dorset/
Rambouillet/Finn
Fleece weight: 7–11 lbs.
Staple length: 3"–5"
Fiber diameter: 22–29 microns
Lock characteristics: Pointed tips;
may have unorganized crimp
Color: White

Rambouillet

Origin: Spanish Merino
Fleece weight: 8–18 lbs.
Staple length: 2"–4"
Fiber diameter: 18–24 microns
Lock characteristics: Square and
blocky
Color: White, though sometimes
blacks and grays are available

Romeldale and CVM
(California Variegated Mutant)

Origin: New Zealand Romney/
Rambouillet cross (possibly with
some long wool in background)
Fleece weight: 6–15 lbs
Staple length: 3"–6"
Fiber diameter: 21–25 microns
Lock characteristics: Tips may be
slightly tapered rather than flat;
crimp and fine fiber diameter typical
of other fine wools
Color: White and multi

Targhee

Origin: Rambouillet/Corriedale/
Lincoln
Fleece weight: 10–14 lbs.
Staple length: 3"–5"
Fiber diameter: 22–25 microns,
but can be up to 28
Lock characteristics: Blocky lock
with somewhat pointed tips
Color: White

Merino

Washing Techniques for Fine Wools

I use two different washing methods for fine wools, choosing between them according to whether I plan to flick and spin from the lock, comb the fine fleece, or hand- or drumcard it. Bulk washing methods tend to mix and move the fibers around, and though much lock structure can still be identified, many of the fibers will be misaligned and difficult to realign. This adds to the waste that happens through bulk processing methods, but if I want to hand- or drumcard a fine fleece, then the bulk washing methods described on pages 110–111 work perfectly well. If I want to preserve the lock structure as much as possible in order to flick it and spin from the lock or comb it, I use my "tulle-sausage" method.

THE TULLE-SAUSAGE METHOD

Making tulle sausages is my favorite way to wash fine fleeces. This washing method is adapted from Margaret Stove's book *Merino: Handspinning, Dyeing and Working with Merino and Superfine Wools.* It works great for fine wools or any fleece in which you want to preserve the lock structure. You can purchase inexpensive netting or tulle at craft or fabric stores. The tulle package I describe stabilizes the locks during the washing process. I usually make six to eight of these at a time because that's how many that fit on my small sweater dryer rack. If you're spinning a fine laceweight yarn, these 6 to 8 ounces of wool will give you hours of spinning fun.

Be sure to use a detergent rather than soap, as soap is generally very alkaline and can damage the wool fibers. It's important to keep the pH as close to neutral as possible: less than pH 9 is good; pH 7 is best. (For more on detergents appropriate for washing fleece, including Unicorn Power Scour, see pages 11 and 12.)

STEP 1. Cut a piece of tulle or netting measuring about 16 inches long and three times as wide as the length of the locks you are working with. (Use less wool if your tulle is narrower than 16 inches.)

STEP 2. Take about an ounce of the locks and lay them facing in the same direction (all cut ends or all tip ends aligned) in the center of the tulle. The thickness of this little row of beautiful locks should be no more than the thickness of a deck of cards. It's important not to make the pile much thicker than that, because you want the dirt to wash away easily.

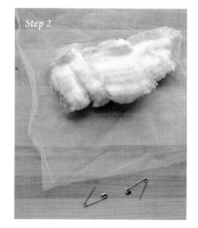

Step 2

STEP 3. Fold over the top and bottom of the tulle and roll in the sides. Use a safety pin to secure each side. You now have a very neat little wool "sausage" that is easy to handle and move around during washing.

Step 3

STEP 4. Fill up your sink, tub, or other receptacle with very hot water. The water can be just as hot as I can get from the tap when I'm using Unicorn Power Scour, as this detergent doesn't need an extremely high temperature to dissolve the lanolin. If you're using a different scour, the water should be above 140°F (60°C) in order to dissolve the grease. Add your chosen brand of wool wash or liquid detergent to the water.

STEP 5. Lay your little sausages into the basin. You can fold them in half if necessary, and I sometimes even stack them on top of each other.

Step 5

STEP 6. After they've soaked for 15–20 minutes, remove the sausages from the water and squeeze the excess water out: do not wring, just squeeze. Limit the soak to 15–20 minutes so that the water does not begin to cool too much. As the water cools, the lanolin tends to return to the wool and redeposit itself there.

STEP 7. Repeat steps 4–6 once more, then twice more with just clear water. After the second wash, if you feel there is still lanolin left, do another wash using more detergent. The more

lanolin and dirt that is removed, the more smoothly the locks will spin. Residual lanolin will cause the wool to feel sticky.

STEP 8. Remove all of the sausages, and squeeze out as much water as possible, then roll them in a towel and squeeze to remove more water. If the water does not run completely clear at this point, it isn't too much of a worry. The main concern here is to remove the lanolin, sweat, and much of the dirt. You'll have another opportunity to get the rest of the dirt out when you wash the skeins after spinning the yarn.

STEP 9. Let them dry on a screen, sweater dryer rack, or towel on a table or the floor.

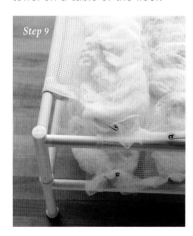

Step 9

THE TULLE-SAUSAGE METHOD, Continued

ENSURING CLEAN FLEECE

Sometimes I find I haven't added enough soap, there's more grease than I thought, or the water I used wasn't hot enough, and so the grease hasn't been completely removed. This makes the locks feel sticky when spinning, and the fibers don't glide past each other easily when I'm drafting. When this happens, I just scour one more time, and it generally gets out the rest of the grease.

You may have heard or read that if the water temperature isn't the same for every wash and rinse, the fleece will felt. This is not a worry. Here are two precautions against felting you should take, however:

- **Agitation.** Avoid too much agitation. Some movement will happen as you change the water and squeeze excess water from the wool, but once the wool is in for a soak, avoid swishing it around in the water.

- **Hot to cold transitions.** Ensure that the water you add to each subsequent wash or rinse is the same temperature or hotter than the water you just drained off. Hot water opens the scales on the wool; cold water causes them to draw in. Going from hot water to cold will full the fibers a bit, but you'll have nothing to worry about if you keep the temperature the same or hotter as you proceed.

Yarns with Bounce

The yarns spun from fleeces in the fine-wool category obviously vary from breed to breed in feel, but I find that what they all have in common is that 3-ply yarns are most definitely more elastic than 2-ply yarns. This isn't the case in every fleece category, but it is so across the board with the fine wools. This holds true regardless of whether the yarn was spun with a woolen or worsted drafting method.

THE LOCK-BY-LOCK METHOD

The lock-by-lock method is another technique for washing fine wools that comes from Margaret Stove. It's surprising how fast this washing can go — just as fast as wrapping all the locks in tulle and washing the packages. I may not choose to do enough for a sweater this way, but I certainly would do 6 to 8 ounces at a time for a lace project.

STEP 1. Fill two small buckets or bowls with hot water: one for wetting the locks and one for rinsing them.

STEP 2. Dip a lock into the hot water and then scrub each end on a laundry detergent bar such as Fels Naptha. This can be a bit scary. We all know how easily these fine wools can felt, and so all of this rubbing seems dangerous. The reason the fibers don't felt is that soap surrounds each one and protects it from rubbing against its neighbors. That's the happy part of this method.

STEP 3. After each end is scrubbed, dip the lock into the rinse bucket. Now is the time for a bit of caution: no scrubbing now, as there's no more protective lanolin or soap coating the fibers to stop felting from happening.

STEP 4. Roll the lock in a towel, squeeze out the water, and lay it flat to dry. These locks will dry surprisingly quickly.

Step 2

Step 3

Step 4

Preparing to Spin Fine Wools

In spinning, for me there's nothing more satisfying than washing a fine fleece and spinning it from the locks to make a beautiful laceweight yarn. The textures and smells are fantastic. I love that it's so much easier to spin wool that you've prepared yourself. You have control over every step, and the outcome is all yours.

I spun all the sample yarns in this chapter from flicked locks, so I won't be discussing the effects of other preps on the yarns spun with fine wools. This shouldn't stop you from carding or combing these fibers, but I am focusing on the preparation method I think works best for each category. I've combed or carded many fine wools; the yarns differ a bit depending on the prep method, but they are all beautiful. As you experiment and sample, you'll find what the differences are. Sampling and swatching are your friends, and as your experience grows, you'll be able to make some educated guesses about how to approach a fleece, even if you've never touched that breed before.

In addition to preparing locks for immediate spinning, by the way, flicking is also a great way to prepare locks for drumcarding or combing, as it opens up the ends and makes the next step a lot easier.

The Pros of Flicking Fine Wools

I love to flick the fine wools for several reasons. First, I love the yarn I get from a flicked lock. This processing method allows the fibers to maintain their alignment, but also to puff up a bit more than they would if they were combed. The yarn that results has great insulating properties, while at the same time it somewhat resembles a smooth, worsted-style yarn. In addition, I usually use the finer wools for lighter-weight projects such as scarves and shawls where I need less than 12 ounces of clean wool. Flicking allows me to sit in the living room in front of my wheel and flick a little, then spin a little, as the process takes up very little space. Finally, I like flicking fine wools (especially those at the finest end of the fine-wool spectrum) because they have a tendency to develop neps when hand- or drumcarded, unlike when flicked.

Equipping Yourself to Flick

A flick card is small tool with a handle and rectangular or square piece of wood with carding cloth attached. (For more information about flick cards, see pages 16–17.) Some people like to wear a glove on the hand that holds the fiber when they're flicking. I understand this because I generally can't help hitting a knuckle or two accidentally while flicking. I rarely wear a glove or other protection, however, because I have a hard time holding all of the fibers. Also, I get a lot more waste when I wear a glove, so I risk bare hands every time.

It's important to have some kind of covering on your leg to protect yourself and your clothing from the carding pins. A piece of leather is nice, and it will wear well for a very long time. You can get a piece of leather from a tack store or other leather supply company.

Rather than the supple leather used in clothing, choose instead something with some body and a little thickness that you can lay comfortably across your knee.

I use a lap cloth made of two thicknesses of canvas. Although the pins of the flick have damaged the cloth some, it has lasted for more than three years. My lap cloth has a white side and a black side, which also serves me well as a background when I'm spinning. I use the white side when spinning dark fibers and the black side when spinning lighter-colored fibers.

Opening the Lock

There are two ways to open the lock nicely so it will be easy to spin. The first is to use a tapping or bouncing motion; the second is more like combing. Whichever method you use, never try to work with a large amount of fleece at a time. Something about the thickness of your thumb is usually best.

THE TAPPING OR BOUNCING METHOD

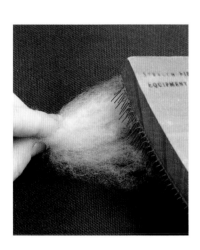

STEP 1. Take the fibers and hold one end of the lock over your knee with your lap cloth in place for protection. With the flick, begin to gently tap the ends of the fibers. You will see the fibers begin to spread and open.

STEP 2. Turn the lock over so the underside is up, and again gently tap the fibers with the flick.

STEP 3. After the fibers are sufficiently open at one end, take the other end of the lock in your fingers, and follow steps 1 and 2 to open it in the same way.

THE BRUSHING METHOD

This technique is more of a brushing motion, and I prefer this approach to tapping or bouncing, maybe because it's gentler on my knee. There is a bit more waste with it, as many of the shorter and weaker fibers are removed in the process of brushing. I really think it gets the job done a little faster, however, and I like the results better.

STEP 1. Take a lock, again about the thickness of your thumb, and put a little twist in the center of it. The twist holds the fibers in place as you flick. Hold that area of twist as you brush the lock.

STEP 2. Draw the flick through the lock at one end a couple of times, then turn the lock around and repeat on the other end.

STEP 3. When both ends are open, grab them and wiggle them back and forth to open the center. You now have a rectangular-shaped lock.

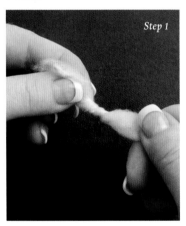
Step 1

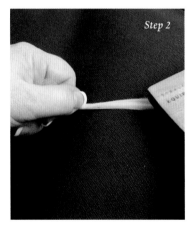
Step 2

Step 3

Spinning Flicked Locks

Place a lock in the crook of your hand and spin, beginning at the tip of your thumb. I have found that a short forward draw works best to get a lovely, smooth laceweight yarn. The fibers just happily follow each other in an orderly way from the beginning of the lock to the end. Sometimes as I get close to the last bit of the lock, the fibers have become a little disorganized, resulting in yarn that's less consistent and less smooth than I like. At that point, I stop spinning that lock and either just discard it or put it in my basket to be carded later.

You may wonder whether to spin from the tip end or the cut end. My advice is to spin from whichever end you feel comfortable with, but for the best yarn, be consistent throughout the project. I have always spun from the cut end, because of the direction that the scales on the fiber grow. For me, spinning from the cut end feels smoother and easier. Margaret Stove has always spun from the tip, and she is a genius with fine wools and lace spinning. It's entirely up to you.

Don't be afraid to experiment. Wool is your friend. If you mess up a few little sausages, it's only an ounce or two. You can chalk it up to a great learning experience — plus the sheep are growing more wool for you right now.

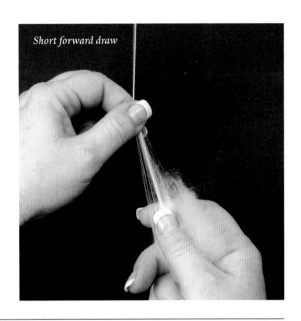

Short forward draw

Keeping Track of Lock Direction

Many times I do all of this prep right at my spinning wheel and spin each lock as soon as I finish opening it. Instead, you can flick the locks all at once, if you prefer, and put them in a basket or other container to be spun at another time. If you decide to do the flicking all at once and then do all the spinning afterward, you should line the locks up in a box so that they are all facing the same direction: cut ends one way and tip ends the other.

With some wools, it can be difficult to tell which is the tip and which is the cut end after flicking. Here's a little trick to help you decide which end is which: Hold the lock between your thumb and forefinger and begin moving your thumb in an up-and-down motion across the lock and your finger. The lock should begin to move. The end that is coming nearer to your fingers is the tip end.

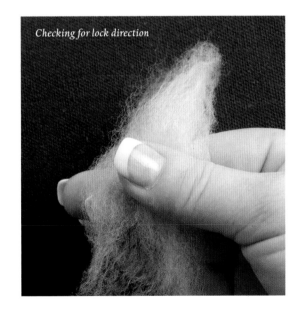

Checking for lock direction

MERINO

Merino fleece is the standard by which most other wool fibers are measured. Merino has been bred for consistency over the whole fleece. The fiber diameters, crimp, and length at the neck of the fleece should be similar to the fiber diameters, crimp, and length at the back end of the fleece. There are at least 15 different strains of Merino worldwide. The fineness, body style, and breeding characteristics can vary widely, depending on what the shepherd wants to get out of his flock. These characteristics include finer wool, or more multiple births in the flock, or heavier fleece weight, or a sheep that will thrive in certain climates.

A well-known characteristic of Merino is the fineness of the breed's fibers. The fibers

unwashed Merino fleece

found across all of these strains range from 11.5 microns to 26 microns, with most falling in the 20 to 25 micron range. In the past, some wool-fineness grading systems were even calibrated on how much Merino was included in a breed. Grading systems now in use are based on the grade or thickness of wool, and no longer take into account the amount of Merino in the breed's background (see Understanding Wool Grading Systems on the opposite page). The consistency throughout the fleece that is found in Merino and many of the other breeds in the fine wools category isn't found in all breeds, however, which is what makes Merino such a good wool to compare with other breeds.

The Challenges of Processing Merino

Merino can be difficult to process, as the fibers are sometimes tender and delicate. In much of the commercially processed Merino, its characteristic crimp and resilience may have been negatively affected by chemical processing to remove vegetable matter and dirt, or another of the many machine-processing steps that can be hard on fibers. Processed Merino is extremely easy to find for handspinning, however.

Merino has its beauties and its drawbacks for handspinners. Here are the things to love about it, processed or not: It is soft; we all love soft things. Due to its accessibility, it is relatively inexpensive. It's available in many colors — hand-dyed, industrially dyed, multicolored, and solids. You can find a Merino for practically any project or idea you can think of, but Merino is not necessarily the right fiber for every project. It is extremely fine, which makes it also not as hard-wearing as you might like for certain items. The fibers can be short, which means it needs more twist or it will pill.

One of the more major frustrations with Merino is that it is not the easiest fiber to spin consistently. Various tricks can help (see Tips for Spinning Consistent Yarn below), but even if you follow these tips, Merino sometimes does not wish to cooperate with your goal of a consistent, smooth yarn, especially the pulling-out-the-same-number-of-fibers part. It likes to clump up, to invite more friends to the party than there is room for in that particular part of the yarn. This is not true of all fine wools, but, in my experience, it's true of Merino most of the time. Granted, I have not tried all the many strains of Merino; in fact, I probably haven't been able to get my hands on more than two

Tips for Spinning Consistent Yarn

A spinner has plenty of ways to get a more consistent yarn, including the following:

- Treadle at a steady speed.
- Draft in rhythm with your treadling.
- Draft a consistent length, pulling out the same amount of fibers with each draft.
- Create a 3- or 4-ply yarn to even out the thin and thick spots in the singles and create a rounder yarn.

Understanding WOOL GRADING SYSTEMS

The count, or grade, refers to the hanks of yarn, each 560 yards long, that can theoretically be spun from 1 pound of wool top. A 64s wool yields 35,840 yards (560 times 64) of yarn from 1 pound of 64s top.

The U.S. Department of Agriculture (USDA) wool grading system takes into account only the average fiber thickness of a fleece. Fiber thickness is currently measured with computer imaging, but in the past a microscope was the most common measuring tool. Whichever method is used, several hundred separate fibers are measured to get an accurate average. In addition, the fibers in the sample cannot vary more than a certain percentage from the average.

For example, if the average micron count of a sample is 25 microns, the standard deviation must be no more than 7.06 microns to be placed in the grade of 58s. (In simple terms, standard deviation means that a certain amount of these fibers can't vary more than 7.06 microns on either side of the average.) In this example, therefore, there will be some fibers that are 32 microns as well as some that are 18 microns, but the majority fall in the area of 25 microns. If the standard deviation is more than what is called for at each level, the wool may be labeled to fall within two categories, such as 58–60s, instead of just 58s.

Notice that this grading system takes into account only the fiber diameter. Grading by crimp alone is not done, as there is not a perfect relationship between the crimp in a fiber and the fiber's diameter; for our purposes, though, it can give us a starting point for deciding how a particular fleece can be spun to its strengths. (For more about using crimp to guide spinning decisions, see pages 44–45.) The system also does not take into account such other considerations as length, luster, strength, elasticity, hand, or color. All of these things have to do with quality and/or spinnability.

Wool Grades and Micron Counts

GRADE	AVERAGE FIBER DIAMETER (IN MICRONS*)
Finer than 80s	Under 17.70
80s	17.70–19.14
70s	19.15–20.59
64s	20.60–22.04
62s	22.05–23.49
60s	23.50–24.94
58s	24.95–26.39
56s	26.40–27.84
54s	27.85–29.29
50s	29.30–30.99
48s	31.00–32.69
46s	32.70–34.39
44s	34.40–36.19
40s	36.20–38.09
36s	38.10–40.20
Coarser than 36s	Over 40.20

*A micron is a millionth of a meter.

Taken from the United States Standards for Grades of Wool, U.S. Department of Agriculture, 1968.

or three strains, but I've tried the ones that are readily available to spinners in both raw and processed form on a regular basis.

Processing your own Merino makes spinning it a bit easier, but both hand-processed fleece and mill-processed top seem to act in a similar manner. I mention this problem because sometimes when we're spinning and can't get the yarn we want, we blame ourselves. We think we aren't good enough. We're disappointed and get discouraged. If this is the case when you're spinning Merino, work with a different wool for a while and come back to Merino later. I will never say that a spinner can become the master of Merino wool, because it seems to have a mind of its own. You can surely work in a successful partnership with this wool, however, as your hands learn how to support and move with its fibers.

If you decide to experiment with another fine-wool breed instead, there are lots of other fibers with a similar crimp structure and fiber diameter that would be happier to comply with the things you ask of them. One suggestion is Rambouillet, a Merino strain with a fine fiber diameter but with a more resilient crimp structure, which adds bounce and warmth as well as makes it easier to spin a more consistent yarn.

Romeldale/California Variegated Mutant (CVM) is another great choice. This breed has a fantastic, fine crimp similar to Merino, due its Rambouillet genetics, but it's easier to

spin consistently. I attribute this cooperative nature to the Romney in its background. This breed is listed by The Livestock Conservancy as Critical, which means there are fewer than 200 annual registrations of the breed and fewer than 2,000 animals of the breed exist worldwide. Purchasing and spinning the wool from these sheep will encourage shepherds to keep them and raise them, and therefore help save this American breed. It's not currently readily available in processed form, but try contacting shepherds directly to find this as top or roving.

Tracking Down Hard-to-Find Breeds

The best way to find sheep breeders in your area is to go to your state's breeders' association website. In my case, this is the Michigan State Sheep Breeders Association; most states have their own. Another good option is the U.S. Sheep Breeders Online Directory website, which has been a great help to me when I can't find the breed I want within my state.

Another tactic that has worked for me when I'm trying to find fleeces is simply to stop at a sheep farm when I am out and about. My enthusiasm for the sheep and their wool is usually a great introduction, and it often gives me a chance to talk face to face with the shepherd about what he or she is doing.

Sampling Merino

In spite of the difficulties of spinning this breed, I have to say that a well-spun Merino yarn makes a luscious fabric. Due to its shorter staple length, I prefer to ply my Merino yarns. The plying not only adds strength but also tucks in more ends, which reduces pilling. The more plies, the more the pilling is reduced. I love a 3- or 4-ply Merino yarn. The yarns I have spun as examples shown here are all 2- or 3-ply yarns spun either with no twist in the fiber supply (worsted) or by allowing twist to enter the fiber supply (woolen).

❶ 3-ply worsted-spun. The smoothest yarn is this 3-ply worsted-spun yarn, which is about sock weight. It is slightly elastic and doesn't feel as soft in the skein as you would expect from a Merino yarn because I added a bit more twist than you would generally see in a mill-spun Merino yarn. The hand of this skein might put some people off if they were buying this yarn, saw it labeled as Merino, and had different expectations for it. But let's look at the magic. The fine-gauge swatch I knit with it is very elastic, smooth, and soft, and drapes well. I spent a little time rubbing one corner of the swatch to see how much it might pill, and though on close inspection it appears a bit fuzzier there, it's not apparent when looking at the entire swatch. This isn't to say that this fabric will never pill, but it does demonstrate a good resistance to it.

1 — Merino — flicked/ worsted-spun from cut end/ 3-ply/sock weight

❷ & ❸ 2-ply worsted-spun. The two 2-ply yarns were both spun with a worsted draft and with a similar twist and thickness in the singles. On the opposite page, the one above (2) has more twist added in the ply; the one below (3) has a low twist in the ply. When you examine these yarns in the skeins, you can see that the lower-twist sample shows the spinning inconsistencies more clearly, while some of that is masked in the higher-twist sample.

I wove samples using each of these yarns and found that they are a bit different from each other, though each was woven to the same size and put through the same finishing process. To finish them, I agitated them energetically in hot water and a little soap for about one minute to cause some fulling and filling in of the spaces between the interlacing threads. You can see that after this treatment, the lower-twist sample shows more shrinkage than the higher-twist sample. Both woven samples developed a nice hazy appearance and

softened quite a bit. The higher-twist sample is a bit bouncier and springier than the low-twist sample, though I wouldn't call it elastic. The lower-twist sample has less body and more drape than the sample with higher twist. Both fabrics would be great for a light jacket, shawl, or lined skirt. I say "lined" because there are still some spaces between the yarns. If these yarns were set more closely, the resulting fabric would be great for all sorts of garments.

I also knit a lace swatch using both these yarns. The lace swatch knit with the lower-twist 2-ply yarn has great drape, with the look of a gossamer lace. The hand is a bit softer than the one knit with the higher-twist yarn, and so this would be a great yarn for a lace project that calls for flowing lines, such as a shawl. The lace from the higher-twist 2 ply has more body and a crisper feel. It would be wonderful for lace items that need more structure, such as a lace sweater.

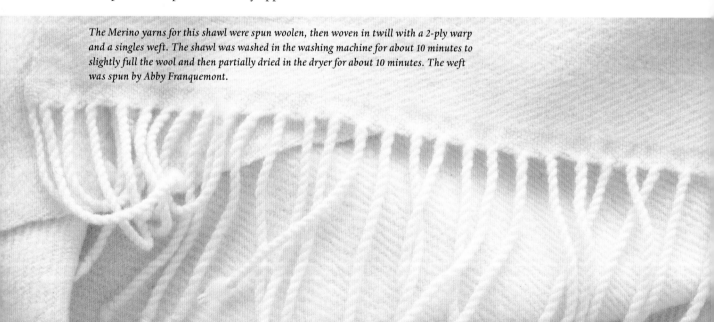

The Merino yarns for this shawl were spun woolen, then woven in twill with a 2-ply warp and a singles weft. The shawl was washed in the washing machine for about 10 minutes to slightly full the wool and then partially dried in the dryer for about 10 minutes. The weft was spun by Abby Franquemont.

2 — *Merino* —
flicked/
worsted/average
twist in singles/
2-ply/high twist

3 — *Merino* —
flicked/
worsted-spun
from cut end/
average twist in
singles/
2-ply/low twist

❹ & ❺ **3-ply woolen-spun.** The 3-ply woolen-spun yarns were spun a bit thicker than any of the worsted-spun yarns, as I was aiming to get warmth from them. I spun sample 5 from the cut end, allowing the twist to enter the fiber supply. This yarn is a bit more elastic than the 2-ply with the lower ply twist (sample 3, previous page), even though their ply twists per inch are about equal. The fact that the fibers are not being stretched and smoothed during the spinning process as happens in worsted spinning is one of the contributing factors to the additional elasticity. The swatch is soft and inviting, but it stands up nicely to the same rubbing and abrasion used on the 3-ply worsted-spun sample.

I spun sample 4 woolen from the fold, allowing twist into the fiber supply. This is the most "woolen-looking" sample: It is fluffy and fuzzy. The yarn has elasticity and the squoosh factor that most knitters look for in the yarn store. If I had all of these yarns lined up on a shelf to choose from, this would be the one I would go for every time. It felt good in my hands when I knit with it. The others did, too, but this was the softest and loftiest. But here is the drawback: When I abraded this swatch, even using less force and taking less time, the fibers began to lift out and pill more than those in the other samples. Though the fabric feels nice, this will be the sweater that looks worn out after just a few wearings. Though this is the yarn I would have reached for to squeeze if I were going to buy yarn, after seeing what happened to it in the swatching, it's the one

4 — *Merino* —
flicked/
woolen-spun
from the fold/
3-ply

I would put right back in favor of something more solidly built. The short-staple fibers combined with the low-twist spinning process at commercial mills cause the pilling in many store-bought Merino yarns. If I'm going to handspin a yarn, I want something with more strength and wearability.

Spinning these short fibers from the fold effectively cuts their length in half, contributing to the pilling factor you would get naturally. Add to that spinning for loft, and you have a pill factory on your hands. Though some other fibers react well to spinning from the fold, these short-stapled fibers (less than 4 inches) are not the best choice for a garment you want to wear for years.

Elastic Sock Yarn from Fine Wools

My favorite method for getting an elastic sock yarn from fine wools is to start with a singles spun with low to average twist. I don't go out of my way to do anything special for the singles, but when I ply, I add more twist than I would if I were trying to spin a naturally balanced yarn. I find that a 40- to 45-degree twist angle is about where I want to be with the ply twist. By using this approach, I take advantage of the natural elasticity stored in the crimp and combine that characteristic with bouncy plying, and, like magic, I have a sock yarn that, when knit, molds to my feet, moving with me rather than swirling around and not staying in place. This method doesn't work for all wools, though. The close crimp of the fine wools is what makes the difference; longwools will never give this effect.

I do prefer more than two plies for socks, however, as the extra plies add strength to the yarn. I also avoid using 100 percent Merino for sock yarn, because I feel that the fine-diameter fiber is not as durable as I would like. When I blend in a little bit of a stronger fiber, however, I can get the best of both worlds. If I blend in a wool to do the job, I might choose Corriedale because its crimp mimics the Merino, and so the elasticity will be similar. A softer Romney fleece will add strength, but some of the elasticity might be lost, since there are somewhat fewer crimps per inch in that fiber. Many people like to blend in a type of rayon, such as bamboo, because it has a fine diameter and thus will cooperate with the wool, but it is also very strong.

5

— *Merino* —
flicked/
woolen-spun
from cut end/
3-ply

CORMO

Cormo was developed in Tasmania by crossing Saxon Merinos with Corriedale sheep. The result was a sheep with a larger body and a wool with beautifully defined crimp and a longer staple length than Merino. The yarns can also have some luster to them, which is rare in fine-wool breeds. I attribute the shine to the Lincoln in this breed's genealogy.

Cormo locks are square with blocky tips. Fleeces can weigh up to 12 pounds, which is usually plenty for at least three adult-size sweaters. This is why finding a few friends to share a Cormo fleece with may be a good idea. Average lock length is 3 to 5 inches, and the fiber diameter ranges from 17 to 23 microns.

Individual fibers from this breed are extremely elastic, sometimes making processing difficult, whether by hand or by machine.

Using a flick will maintain lock structure as well as remove any neps or noils from the lock. Combing is another great option with this breed, but it's important to comb slowly and deliberately so as to avoid adding to the usual waste produced by combing.

Handcarding and drumcarding may add neps, resulting in a textured yarn. The way to avoid these neps is by moving the cards or the handle of the drumcarder much more slowly than you would like. The neps form on a drumcarder because individual fibers get caught on the pins of the licker-in as they are being taken by the main drum. The end of the fiber that is caught on the licker-in then springs off toward the drum and makes a cute little coiled-up knot of fiber; a similar thing happens with handcards. This problem isn't limited to Cormo. It can occur with many of the other fine fibers. The key in carding is to take your time. A fine-toothed drum or fine cloth on your handcards gets the job done in fewer passes, which also helps you avoid neps.

Mill Processing for Your Fine Wools

If you've purchased a Cormo or other fine-wool fleece and wish to have it processed rather than do it yourself, it's important to seek out a mill with experience processing these finer fibers. Instead of requesting carded fleece alone, ordering combed top may give a better processed fiber, as any neps that are formed in the carding process will be removed in that last combing step. This will, however, add some cost to the processing bill. Most mills will give you the combing waste when you get your fleece back. You may want to use these neps for making tweed batts and textured yarns.

Sampling Cormo

Though all the finished yarns from the fine wools have bounce and elasticity, Cormo is the one that always seems most elastic. The twists per inch in my samples show a tight ply twist, although when I was plying, my angle of twist was about 40 degrees, with fewer twists per inch than in the finished yarn. After washing, the skeins shrank in length and the angle of twist decreased. The reason for this is that the fibers are stretched during spinning, and they are then held in place when twist is added.

When the spun yarn is immersed in water, the fibers want to go back to their original crimp. This shortens the length of the skein and affects the angle of twist. You may also be surprised at how thick the finished yarn is, compared to the way it looks on the bobbin. The yarn you're spinning may look like the finest laceweight, but when plied and washed, it fluffs up to two or three times the thickness it appeared to be on the bobbin. Because of the characteristics of this fiber, sampling is especially important.

Though Cormo can be tricky to process, and it may be even trickier to predict the thickness of the resulting yarn, it also has a very sumptuous feel. The combination of elasticity and fineness results in a fabric that can be used for the most luxurious of projects. Knitting with this yarn is almost too pleasurable for me. I have a habit of stopping and rubbing my knitting on my face a little too often while working. Lace made from Cormo makes me stop even more often, and so I make less progress than normal. This fabric has drape as well as spring.

1 Laceweight. Let's begin with what I thought was my favorite yarn to spin from Cormo: laceweight. I spun this yarn from the cut end of a flicked lock using a short forward-draw draft. When under tension, the singles are about as fine as sewing thread.

When plying this breed (and some others with as much bounce and crimp as you see here), it is important to maintain equal tension on both strands. It is very easy for one strand to loosen up and wrap around the other, rather than both wrapping around an invisible core, which is the goal. In addition, when spinning this fine with Cormo, it's important to have enough twist in both the singles and the ply. The fibers really want to spring back into their original crimp pattern, and if there's not enough twist to manage this crimp, the yarn will appear to be wavy (see photo below). This concern about twists per inch may be a real worry only if you are entering the skein in a competition, because if you're using it for a knit lace project, the item will be blocked and the waviness will not be visible. Still, you will want more twist in very finely spun yarn than in a thicker one, simply because twist is necessary to hold the whole thing together. As always, sampling is your friend. And taking the sampling all the way through to the washed swatch always gives you the answers you are looking for about the yarn you are spinning.

Cormo yarn showing waviness because of too-low twist

1 — Cormo —
flicked/
worsted-spun from
cut end with short
forward draw/
2-ply/low twist/
laceweight

❷ 2-ply. I spun the singles for the 2-ply yarn in the woven sample using exactly the same method as I used for the singles in the knitted lace sample, with two differences. One is that the singles for the woven sample is about twice as thick as the singles in the lace sample. The second difference is that the amount of ply twist in the woven sample yarn is about double that of the ply twist in the lace sample. This yarn is so stretchy that it seems like some elastic thread was spun with the yarn. It's amazing! When I warped my loom for sampling, I did not put as much tension on the warp yarns as I generally use with a less-elastic yarn. My goal was to keep that elasticity active. The sample stretches more in the weft direction than in the warp direction, because the weft threads were never stretched at all during the weaving. This brings more questions for me. Would more tension on the warp have given an even more elastic sample off the loom? I finished the sample aggressively in hot water with a bit of Soak (from Soak Wash Inc.) or Fibre Wash (from Unicorn Fibre). The warp and weft yarns moved closer and filled in the holes, but the fabric is smooth and didn't halo like the Merino woven swatches.

2 — *Cormo* — *flicked/ worsted-spun from cut end/ 2-ply/high twist*

❸ 3-ply worsted-spun. Like the 2-ply, I prepared this fleece by flicking it, and then spun with a short forward draw with no twist between my hands. Like the 3-ply yarn, the knitted sample is very beautiful to look at. The only drawback is that there's a bit more twist in the singles than I would like, which means that the yarn feels a little harder than I prefer with Cormo. If it were any other breed, I would probably be very happy with it, but I want to conserve the extreme softness of this fleece, and since what I have in my mind is to knit a sweater with it, I want it to be next-to-skin soft.

I plied using the same size whorl as I used to spin the singles. Since I'm a little unhappy with the texture of this yarn, I'll make another sample using a slower whorl for the plying to see if the yarn softens up a bit. If that doesn't work, I'll try putting a lower twist in the singles.

Because of its very fine fiber diameter, this Cormo worsted-spun is not the wool I would choose for socks, but it would make a great cardigan. Its fiber length combined with plying will make a yarn that pills a lot less than a shorter-stapled Merino with the same softness, and the Cormo has extra bounce built in.

3 — Cormo — flicked/worsted-spun from cut end with short forward draw/3-ply

❹ & ❺ Woolen-spun. As I said before, I thought laceweight was my favorite yarn to spin from Cormo, but these woolen yarns were a huge surprise in all ways. The stretchier yarn (4) is from flicked locks spun woolen from the fold. This yarn is soft and bouncy and makes me want to sleep with it. The fabric from this yarn is also very stretchy and feels like an everyday sweater. I spun the other yarn (5) woolen from the cut end of a flicked lock. Although there is very little difference in the appearance of these yarns, the yarn spun from the fold is a touch more elastic.

Both yarns are a bit more liable to pill than a worsted-spun yarn. Rubbing the swatches with my finger in one spot for about a minute worked some of the fibers to the top. I have found that fabrics made with longer-stapled fibers seem to pill for a certain period of time, and then, once those loose fibers have worked their way out, the pilling comes almost to a halt. Wools with a staple that is shorter than 4 inches may never stop pilling, but it will be reduced over time. Make a sample, carry it in your pocket for a while, and see what happens. As with all sampling, this can be a learning experience, and eventually it may not be necessary to go through all of these steps when you return to the same wool.

The Search for Softness

When you're looking for next-to-skin softness *and* durability with very little pilling, you may need to choose a fleece with a longer staple length than you find in most of the fine wools. A longer staple length allows for a wider range of twists and therefore may offer the softness and/or durability you are thinking of.

5 — Cormo —
*flicked//
woolen-spun
from cut end/
3-ply*

4 — Cormo —
*flicked/
woolen-spun from
the fold/
3-ply*

POLYPAY

Polypay sheep were developed in Idaho by a
shepherd named Reed Hulet, who needed to
make a profit on his ranch. After some thought
and research, he and his brother, Clarence
Hulet, who was a researcher in Idaho for the
USDA, began to cross four breeds of sheep that
they thought would give them animals with
good body size, more lambs, and great wool
for both handspinning and mechanical processing. The brothers began working toward their
goal in 1968, and by 1970, the first four-breed
lambs were born. These new composite sheep
were named Polypay in 1975, and the American
Polypay Sheep Association formed in 1980.
The Hulets called their new breed Polypay
to emphasize the fact that there are multiple
income streams possible from this breed.

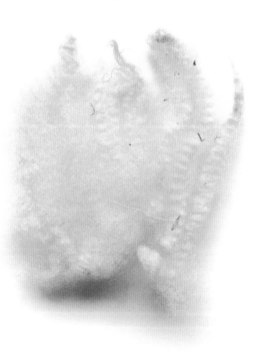

Sampling Polypay

Although the locks of Polypay sheep do not completely fit my profile of how a fine-wool lock should look, I have placed Polypay in the fine-wools category because of its other characteristics, which are typical. Its crimp is well defined and consistent from butt to tip; fibers have about 6 to 9 crimps per inch in the lock. The staple length of 3 to 5 inches is consistent with what we would consider normal for a fine wool. The fiber also behaves similarly to other fine-wool breeds when you process and spin it. The one difference is Polypay's lock structure. Whereas fine wools generally have blocky tips to their locks, Polypays have a somewhat tapered tip. In addition, yarns and fabrics of Polypay wool are a lot more durable than other wools in this category.

I flicked all of the locks for the four Polypay yarns and five samples shown here, and then spun from the locks in varying ways. Not surprisingly, there's much more luster in the worsted-spun yarns. I was surprised, however, by how different the worsted- and woolen-spun yarns look from each other. The worsted- and woolen-spun Merino yarns also look and feel different from one another, but you have to be very perceptive to *see* the differences, whereas the *feel* is very obvious. With Polypay, on the other hand, the differences are clear at a glance, and no handling is required to distinguish between them.

❶ & ❷ 2- and 3-ply worsted-spun. These yarns were worsted-spun with a short forward draw. I spun both from the cut end of the lock; one is a 2-ply and the other a 3-ply. It was easy to get a smooth, fine, and fairly consistent yarn when I spun these samples worsted.

The 3-ply (2) yarn is drapey, with a lovely, soft hand and plenty of luster. The knitted swatch from this yarn is also drapey and delightfully elastic. I could see using it for a fine-gauge sweater that could be worn next to the skin. This yarn would also be beautiful for a cabled knit or for use in colorwork. Everything would pop.

The 2-ply (1) yarn perhaps could have used a tiny bit less twist in the ply, but it looks beautiful and feels very crisp in the hand. The lace knit from this yarn confirmed that I would have preferred a bit less twist in the ply in order to get more drape and softness, although the holes want to stay open and visible.

I finished the woven sample by agitating it by hand for at least a minute in hot, soapy water. Though there was a bit of shrinkage, there wasn't a lot. The finished fabric looks very similar to the unwashed sample. I suspect that the fact that it fulled very little after finishing is because of the higher twist in the ply. This sample is also crisp feeling, with great body.

1 — *Polypay* —
flicked/
worsted-spun
from the cut end
with short forward
draw/
2-ply

2 — *Polypay* —
flicked/
worsted-spun
from cut end with
short forward
draw/
3-ply

❸ & ❹ 3-ply woolen-spun. I plied both of the woolen samples to a 3-ply yarn. I spun sample 3 from the cut end of the lock, allowing twist to enter the fiber supply. I made this woolen-spun singles slightly thicker than the worsted-spun singles, but only slightly. When it came time to ply and finish the yarn, it bloomed magically. No fancy finishing was needed. Just a soak in the hot water and the yarn appeared to be almost twice the thickness it was before washing. The swatch has body, but at the same time, it is soft. This reminds me of that sweater you want to put on for chilly evenings at home.

I flicked the locks for sample 4, and then spun them from the fold, allowing twist into the fiber supply as I spun. This denser yarn is appropriate for an outdoor sweater. I spun the singles to approximately the same size as the other woolen-spun sample, but I put more twist in the ply this time, which should both increase its durability and decrease the pill factor.

This yarn was a bit more difficult to spin consistently. In the fold, the fibers seemed to want to bring all of their friends along in groups. When this happens, you've got to do something counter-intuitive: Softer hands and a more open grip will give you a more consistent yarn. Gripping more tightly will just make those fibers fight harder to get through, resulting in lumpy, bumpy yarns. And while that is sometimes your goal, it is important to know how to control things so that the yarns you are making are purposeful, not accidental.

Both swatches knit with the woolen-spun yarns have similar elasticity, and both are inviting. In addition to garments made from this

A Story of Developing a Breed

The Hulet brothers chose the following breeds and crosses to develop Polypay:

- Finnsheep (aka Finnish Landrace or just Finn), which are known for having multiple births with a short gestation period, were crossed with Rambouillet sheep, which have a nice, heavy fleece.

- Dorsets with good body size, which had been born as twins or triplets, were crossed with Targhee, a newer breed that had been developed for good body size and lovely fleece.

The sheep from these two crosses were then crossed with each other. The resulting sheep mature quickly, have short gestational periods, and tend to have multiple births. Polypays produce two lamb crops per year. These combined features help a shepherd get more return on investment and have a more profitable farm.

In addition to these assets, Polypays have one wool crop per year of a very beautiful, dense, heavy fleece, desirable for handspinning and the wool industry. The most desirable traits from each ancestor breed come through in the fleece: there is the bounce of the Dorset, the spongy feel from the Targhee, the fineness of the Rambouillet, and a bit of shine from the Finn.

wool, I could see home-decoration items as well as blankets from this woolen-spun yarn.

After working with Polypay, I have so many more ideas for this fiber. For instance, I think combing it would bring out even more of its natural luster. I'd like to try spinning the same singles from a combed prep, and see how it reacts, as well as compare its ply twist with that of the flicked-prep yarns. The beautiful wool of this modern sheep, originally bred for multiple uses, is now being overlooked in favor of giving the breed just a meat focus. I hope that shepherds and handspinners begin to see the benefits of using this wool.

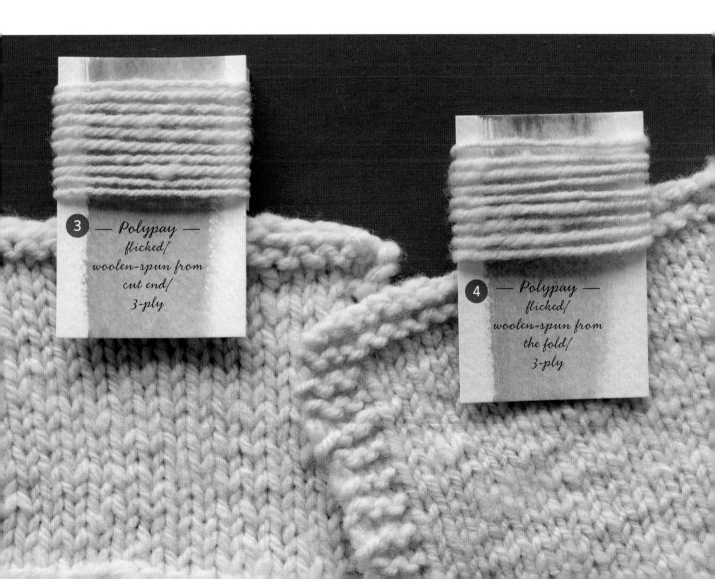

3 — Polypay —
flicked/
woolen-spun from
cut end/
3-ply

4 — Polypay —
flicked/
woolen-spun from
the fold/
3-ply

CORRIEDALE

Corriedale is a wool that is often taken for granted or overlooked when people are considering something to use for a sweater, shawl, or scarf. This may be because it's not as sexy as something a little finer or more exotic.

The earliest breeding that led to Corriedale occurred on New Zealand's South Island, although several shepherds were apparently thinking the same thoughts and crossing the same breeds for similar outcomes all over Australia and New Zealand. The magical cross was Merino and Lincoln, which resulted in a sheep with great wool as well as good body weight; it is also adaptable to a wider variety of pastures than either of its parents. The breed

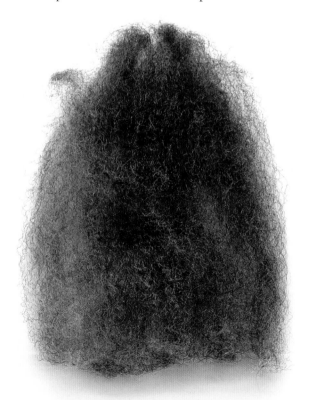

that resulted from these crosses was eventually called Corriedale, although it wasn't officially named until almost 40 years after the breeding began. Corriedales are now one of the most numerous breeds around the world. Many processed fibers and yarns available to spinners, including Falkland and Punta, are made up of a large amount of Corriedale wool, even though they're not labeled that way.

Many people think of Corriedale as a medium wool, and for good reason: the micron range of its fiber (25 to 35 microns) places this wool firmly in the medium range. I put Corriedale into the fine-wools category, however, because of its crimp pattern and lock structure, in spite of its usual micron count, which is on the outer edge of fine. Medium wool often gets overlooked, in my opinion, because medium makes us think of just average or not special. The fine crimp pattern of this breed brings a bounce and spring to the yarn. The thicker diameter adds strength and durability to the objects made with the yarn. With this combination, it could certainly be a favorite of a lot of people.

In addition to these wonderful properties, individual fleeces can vary widely, as you can see from the range of fiber diameters. This means that if you search, you can find a fleece perfect for whatever you have in mind, even within the same flock. Some fleeces would be great for next-to-skin wear, and some will work for harder-wearing garments and even household items, like rugs. Even though there is such

a range of fiber diameter within the breed, individual Corriedale fleeces are very consistent in crimp and lock length over the entire fleece, which can make sorting almost unnecessary (for information about sorting, see page 9).

Sampling Corriedale

I realize it's impossible to know how great these yarns feel just from these photographs, but try to imagine how bouncy and squooshy they are. Even though they don't have the bounce and elasticity of Cormo, the stretchiness they do have is important to the resilience of garments made from this wool.

I flicked all of the locks for these samples, and then spun them in varying ways from the lock. Instead of washing the locks in tulle sausages as with the Merino and Cormo (see page 68), I washed batches of about 1 pound each in a tub. This washing method does not keep the locks arranged, so I had a bit more waste than I like as I got them all lined up for flicking.

The staple length of Corriedale averages between 3 and 6 inches, and the locks on this particular fleece were about 5 inches. This is a good length for tucking the ends in enough to avoid pilling and without needing a lot of twist, which makes the wool wiry.

❶ 2-ply worsted-spun. I spun the yarns for the two swatches exactly the same way, by flicking and then spinning from the cut end of the lock using a worsted draft. I used this 2-ply worsted-spun yarn in a woven swatch as well as for a knitted lace pattern. The lace is crisp, with beautiful, open holes. Even though my sample loom produced a very open weave, the woven sample has great body and would be lovely as a jacket or skirt that calls for a bit of structure.

❷ & ❸ 3-ply woolen-spun. I made both of the woolen-spun samples into a 3-ply yarn because I knew I wanted warmth from them, and the 3 ply gives me a nice round yarn that fills in those gaps that a breeze might get through. The sample spun woolen from the lock (2) made this very plump, soft yarn. Very airy and light, it would be great used in knitting or weaving with equally beautiful results. I spun the other sample (3) from the fold after flicking, also with a woolen draft. It's a bit smoother and doesn't have as much of a halo as the other, so the cable pattern really shows nicely. Both of these yarns would be a great next-to-skin choice, and each would also wear very well.

Bond: A Related Breed

Bond sheep were developed in Australia in 1909 by Thomas Bond, using the same breeds the Corriedale breeders were using. His choices, however, were based on the fineness of wool. Bond fleeces appear similar to Corriedale, but they are generally finer overall, with a micron range of 22 to 28 microns. They also have, on average, a longer staple length and heavier fleece weight.

1
— Corriedale —
flicked/
worsted-spun
from cut end/
2-ply

2
— Corriedale —
flicked/
woolen-spun
from cut end/
3-ply

3
— Corriedale —
flicked/
woolen-spun
from the fold/
3-ply

Chapter 5

LONGWOOLS

EUROPEAN FIGURINES resembling longwool-type sheep and dating from the second century offer some evidence that sheep with long locks and this body type were imported to England during the Roman occupation (about 43 to 430 CE). More evidence comes from a few centuries later in the Luttrell Psalter, an illuminated manuscript written and illustrated in Lincolnshire in the early 1300s. It contains detailed drawings of what could be longwool-type sheep, thought to be old-style Lincolns.

Lincoln and Leicester sheep, whose backgrounds crisscross a bit, are the foundation that many other breeds are built on. Some of the breeds I feature in this category are true longwool sheep, but I've also included others not usually termed longwools. The longwool sheep in their backgrounds has added shine and length to their fleeces, as well as the body bulk needed for meat production.

The locks of most longwools are 6 inches or more, with beautiful luster. The crimp structure varies somewhat from breed to breed. Wensleydales and Teeswaters have long locks that hang separately in a sort of spiral curl that is sometimes compared to dreadlocks. The coarse fleeces of the Leicester group have more of a wave, comparable to those pin-curled hairstyles of the 1920s.

Romneys are part of the longwools group because of their genealogy. Their fleece has a crimp similar in pattern to the crimp of the fine wools, although with fewer crimps per inch, more like other longwools, which average 3 to 6 crimps per inch, no matter what shape the crimps are. The lock tips are generally pointed, as with the other longwools.

The longwool category is different from other categories in the range of fiber diameters within it (from 24 microns all the way up to 41 microns). This feature also makes these fleeces very attractive to many spinners. On the fine end, we've got Bluefaced Leicester, which is rarely questioned as a fiber suitable for next-to-skin wear. But the category also includes Lincoln, one of the coarsest of wools. It would not generally be used for garments, unless a fleece is handpicked for that purpose. You may happily come upon a ewe who is on the fine end of the wool spectrum, or maybe a lamb fleece is available.

Fleece from the longwools is dense and heavy. When spinning their first longwool, many spinners are surprised at how much less length they get compared to the same amount of a fine wool. Compare the 1-ounce samples of the unspun fine-wool and longwool fleeces in the photo below, and notice how much loftier the fine wool is. This means that the wool is less dense and lighter. The higher weight/lower volume of the longwools will translate into less length per ounce when compared to finer wools. Plan accordingly when making calculations about how much fiber to buy for a project. For example, a fine wool can lose up to half its weight after washing due to dirt and high grease content. Longwools don't lose as much, usually more like one-quarter to one-third, as they have a bit less grease than the fine wools group. Because of the density of the longwools, however, it's important for a spinner to estimate more fiber when calculating

what's needed. The finished objects will weigh more than comparable projects made with a fine-wool or Down type. Be sure to sample!

These wools also have a tendency to halo, similar to what you would expect from mohair. Even with all of the smoothing and compacting that happens when you draft a worsted yarn, the halo will eventually appear with use, another important reason to sample. Carry a swatch in your pocket for a few days to see how the fabric might change over time and to determine whether it will truly work for your intended purpose.

Avoiding Stereotypes

I cringe when I hear any wool automatically classified as a rug wool. While it's true that some fibers are extremely coarse and perfect for this use, I resist the tendency to hear the name of a certain breed and thoughtlessly judge it as not useful for clothing. Most wools can be used for some sort of clothing, and all wools have benefits for certain uses. I have heard many times, for instance, that Wensleydale is good only for rugs, and while I wouldn't describe it as a fiber I would use for certain undergarments, I would definitely make a cardigan, a lace shawl, or even a scarf from this wool. The secret is to choose well and then process and spin based on the desired end result.

Longwools lend themselves beautifully to worsted preparations and drafting methods. The worsted prep removes the shorter fibers and aligns the remaining fibers. The worsted drafting

(LEFT) *One ounce scoured Wensleydale*
(RIGHT) *One ounce scoured Cormo*

method allows every fiber to stay in line and makes a dense yarn that takes advantage of all the light, so the natural luster can do its magic.

On the other hand, a woolen prep and spinning technique can add warmth to these wools, although you do give up some of the luster that they are known for. If you choose to use handcards or a drumcarder to process these wools, it's important to choose a fleece with locks shorter than 5 or 6 inches. Handcarding long-stapled wools can be very difficult, even ending up in a tangled mess. And long locks can be difficult to remove from a drumcarder, as they are likely to wrap around the drum.

Appreciating Yarn Differences

Because of the luster and tendency to halo, as well as the lower number of crimps per inch of the longwools, differences in spinning methods really matter. When placed next to one another, it is very easy to distinguish between a yarn spun with a woolen draw and one spun

Deciding the Amount of Twist

Using a lower twist in yarns spun with longwool fleece makes them more comfortable for garments. The lower twist also highlights the luster and drape, and prominently displays the natural silkiness of these fibers. On the other hand, more twist makes an extremely strong yarn, which can be difficult to break with your hands. This can be useful when making carpets, bags, or any other item that needs to stand up to a lot of wear and tear.

with a worsted draw, based on the changes in luster and loft in the samples. The differences become even more obvious when the samples are made into knitted or woven fabrics.

Tips for Spinning the Longwools

Longwool fleeces can be a bit more slippery than those in some of the other categories, so here are some suggestions to help you feel more control.

- **Observe the distance between your hands.** I ask new spinners to hold their hands about one-and-a-half staple lengths apart. This is because beginners have a tendency to hold onto everything with an extremely tight grip. Moving your hands apart allows fibers room to slide past each other. As you become more comfortable and loosen your grip, you can move your hands closer together, have a bit more control, and keep the fibers organized.

- **Loosen the wheel's take-up.** Because of their slipperiness, longwool fibers seem to want to drift apart quickly if you have too much take-up (aka, too tight a tension). Loosening the tension gives you time to draft without having to tighten your grip on the fiber. A tight grip generally results in a less-consistent yarn . . . and spinners with sore hands.

- **Draft slowly.** As with all fibers, when I spin worsted, I draft no more than half the staple length of the wool I'm working with. For woolen spinning, I do a lot of sampling to make sure that my drafting is slow enough to get enough twist in the wool for the project I'm working on.

Characteristics of the THE LONGWOOLS

Bluefaced Leicester

Origin: Border Leicester selected for blue faces and fine wool
Fleece weight: 2–5 lbs.
Staple length: 3"–6"
Fiber diameter: 24–28 microns
Lock characteristics: Very thin, fine curly crimp
Color: Usually white

Border Leicester

Origin: Dishley Leicester/Teeswater or Cheviot
Fleece weight: 8–12 lbs.
Staple length: 4"–10"
Fiber diameter: 30–40 microns
Lock characteristics: Tight, lustrous curls
Color: White, blacks, grays

English Leicester
(aka Leicester Longwool)

Origin: Dishley Leicester
Fleece weight: Up to 18 lbs.
Staple length: 6"–10"
Fiber diameter: 32–40 microns
Lock characteristics: Long, lustrous, wavy
Color: White, black, blue gray

Coopworth

Origin: Border Leicester/Romney
Fleece weight: 8–18 lbs.
Staple length: 5"–8"
Fiber diameter: 30–39 microns
Lock characteristics: Long, lustrous
Color: White, grays

Cotswold

Origin: Native to Cotswold region of England with Leicester Longwool
Fleece weight: 8–20 lbs.
Staple length: 7"–15"
Fiber diameter: 33–42 microns
Lock characteristics: Heavy, lustrous
Color: White, black, gray

Gotland

Origin: From Gute sheep in Sweden
Fleece weight: 5½–11 lbs.
Staple length: 7"–15"
Fiber diameter: 18–35 microns, depending on region
Lock characteristics: May be wavy or curly
Color: Grays

Lincoln

Origin: Roman longwools
Fleece weight: 11–16 lbs.
Staple length: 7"–15"
Fiber diameter: 33.5–44 microns
Lock characteristics: Distinct with defined crimp
Color: White, silver grays, maybe browns

Perendale

Origin: Cheviot/Romney
Fleece weight: 7½–11 lbs.
Staple length: 4"–6"
Fiber diameter: 28–37 microns
Lock characteristics: Pointed tips; even, defined crimp
Color: Usually white

Romney

Origin: Romney Marsh/Dishley Leicester
Fleece weight: 8–12 lbs.
Staple length: 4"–8"
Fiber diameter: 29–36 microns
Lock characteristics: Distinct, pointed tips; uniform crimp
Color: Wide range

Teeswater

Origin: Northern England
Fleece weight: 7½–18 lbs.
Staple length: 12"–15"
Fiber diameter: 30–36 microns
Lock characteristics: Long, glowing luster
Color: White (sometimes grays in U.S. upgrades)

Wensleydale

Origin: Dishley Leicester/Teeswater
Fleece weight: 7–10 lbs.
Staple length: 7"–12"
Fiber diameter: 30–36 microns
Lock characteristics: Long, distinct, lustrous
Color: White, grays, blacks

Wensleydale

Washing Longwool Fleece

The longwools, many of which can have a staple length of 6 or more inches in just six months, seem to attract a lot of dirt. Though these fleeces aren't generally greasy, some other issues need to be dealt with in washing, unless the original bearer of the fleece was always kept on a clear, grassy meadow or inside on artificial turf. Because this is an open fleece (meaning that the locks move away from each other all the way down to the skin), dirt, vegetable matter, and other undesirable things can get right down to the root of the fleece. This may sound a bit objectionable, but the open fleece that let that stuff in also easily allows it to leave when you pick, wash, and process it. A hot soak and some detergent often wash these right off the fibers.

Longer fleeces that have been shorn only once a year are beautiful, but they take a bit more work, as there may be areas that have matted. Combing also takes more work, since combing longer fibers makes fiber management a bit more complicated.

Before I begin the washing process, I pick out any large pieces of hay or grass or objectionable areas overlooked in the skirting. If the fleece has irregular length, I sort the parts and keep similar lengths together (for sorting, see page 9). This helps avoid unnecessary waste during combing. Finally, I take the part of the fleece I am about to wash and shake it out over a sheet or a trash container to get out the really loose bits before submerging it in water.

Though I generally comb longwool fleeces, I sometimes wash them in bulk before processing. The locks of a fine-wool fleece can get a bit muddled, but the locks of the longwools can easily be identified and taken from the washed fleece one by one with very little waste.

I wash most of my longwool fleeces in batches of about 8 ounces to 1½ pounds at a time. How much I wash depends on the size of the container I'm using. I don't generally like to wash more than 1½ pounds at a time because the fiber is harder to handle when it's wet. What started out as 1½ pounds turns to 3 pounds when water is added, and that can be a bit unwieldy. Some people like to wash a whole fleece in the bathtub, but I don't like kneeling on the hard floor in a small space, so I came up with a method that works for me.

I use a container small enough to manage when moving it into and out of the sink and dumping out water, but with enough room to completely submerge the fleece in water. The

Wenleydale locks: (TOP) one year's growth; (BOTTOM) 6 months' growth

dirt must have space to separate from the fleece and fall out during the soaking. If the fiber is packed too densely into the container, there won't be enough area for the dirt to move away from the fibers. I like to use a somewhat wide, shallow container so that if I need to take the fleece out with my hands, I'm not in water up to my elbows. A dishpan works well for smaller amounts of fleece (about 8 to 12 ounces).

I make sure to choose a container that's the right size to fit in my washing area. I use three containers at a time in a kind of assembly line. I wash the fleece in all three, then rinse it in all three, before spreading it out to dry on drying screens. This way I can get a whole fleece washed in just a couple of hours.

I don't usually put my fleece in a bag for this process, but some people like to use a lingerie bag, which is designed to wash delicate clothing in the washing machine. The benefit of using a bag is that it supports the fleece and keeps it together so that you don't have to wrestle with it as you move it around during its washes and rinses.

Before you decide to wash an entire fleece this way, make sure you have enough room to spread it out to dry. A fleece needs a lot of room! If you pile it too thickly, it will take forever to dry, especially if it's humid. Your drying fleece should be spread out into one layer about as thick as one staple length at the most.

THE BULK WASHING PROCESS FOR THE LONGWOOLS

STEP 1. Set up three containers, assembly-line fashion, and fill them with water that is around 115°F (46°C) if you are using Power Scour, or hotter than 150°F (65.5°C) if you are using any other scouring agent. Add your choice of cleanser to each container, based on the directions for your chosen scouring agent. Use enough water to cover the fleece and make sure there is enough room for the dirt to escape from the fiber.

STEP 2. Add your wool, but don't overpack the basin. Allow the wool to sink, or push it down gently. Soak 15–20 minutes.

STEP 3. Lift the wool up and squeeze out the water; don't twist it.

Repeat steps 2 and 3 using the next two containers; then repeat these steps again in each of the containers with fresh water that is the same temperature as the first washes, but without using detergent.

Combing the Longwools

Worsted spinning is the perfect method for fleece of the longwool breeds. The length and quality of their fibers call for a tool that can handle their characteristics. If you try to use a flicker, it's sometimes difficult to get to the middle of locks longer than 5 inches. Similarly, cards do not love the length of the fibers, and the process becomes almost unmanageable. Combs, on the other hand, take the entire length of the lock, open it up, and align the fibers beautifully. In addition to being easier to manage on a comb, the worsted prep brings out the natural luster of these fibers and shows it off

---

Spinning Oil Recipes

Spinners use a number of different mixtures as spinning oils or combing milks. Here are a few recipes you can experiment with:

- Combine 1 part rubbing alcohol, 2 parts olive oil, and 7 parts water.

- Add a bit of essential oil to your mixture to make it smell lovely.

- Instead of olive oil, use neatsfoot oil, mineral oil, or baby oil (which contains both mineral oil and lanolin and won't go rancid).

- Combine 1 part Unicorn Fibre Rinse with 5 parts water. This trick, which I learned from my friend Jim Conti, works like a dream, and it also does not go rancid.

- Plain water!

like a beauty queen. Combing removes all of the short fibers and tangled fibers, as well as the second cuts, to make a perfectly smooth, parallel preparation for spinning. The resulting yarn is not only smooth and lustrous but also strong.

Choosing your combs. I describe the various styles of combs in chapter 1 (pages 20–21), but here are some additional tips for which combs to use and how to use them on the longwools. Single-pitch combs are good for a first pass at the fiber; they help remove any large debris and open the fibers a bit to get ready for finer combing. The more rows of tines, the faster the combing goes, because fewer passes are needed to fully prepare the fibers for spinning. If you plan on processing more than one fleece per year, English combs might be a great investment. I have, however, processed pounds and pounds of fiber on my 2-pitch Viking combs.

Spinning oil or combing milk. Before combing, it's a good idea to spritz your fibers with a bit of spinning oil, also sometimes referred to as *combing milk*. This mixture cuts down on static and helps control the fibers, making them easier to comb. It acts a lot like conditioner does for human hair (recipes at the left).

You can add a few drops of the combing milk to the fiber and work it through with your fingers before you load the combs, or spray it directly on the loaded fiber. You need only a small amount to cut down on static electricity and help the combs run smoothly through the fiber. The fibers should not feel at all wet.

Heating your combs. Some spinners like to heat the tines of their combs to make the combing go a bit more smoothly. The warm tines heat the oils in the wool fibers, as well as any water retained by the wool, and the result is a very malleable and yielding fiber mass. To do this, set the tines of the comb on a stove or other heating element, or keep a small pot of hot water nearby.

Take some safety precautions to protect both yourself and your equipment. If you use water, the pot should be shallower than the length of the comb's tines so that the wooden handle is not sitting in the water. Also, make sure to protect the wood of your combs from the direct heat of the stove. The goal is to heat just the metal tines.

If you are combing during the warmer months, heating may not be necessary, but in winter it can be helpful. I don't do this every time I comb, usually because an appropriate heat source is not available. Using a good combing milk can give you the same results. Again, experimenting to find what works best for you is key.

Loading technique. Loading combs is also known as lashing-on. To reduce waste, load locks so as little wool as possible sticks out on the handle side of the tines: less than ¼ inch is optimal. Too much fiber on the back side of the combs means more tangles and less fiber transferred to the other comb, and therefore more waste.

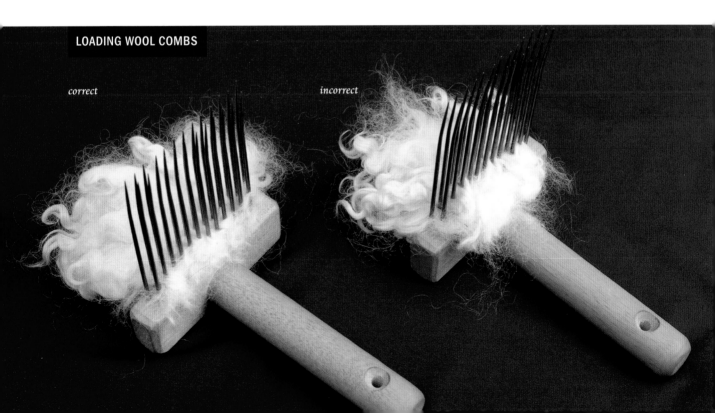

LOADING WOOL COMBS

correct   *incorrect*

I generally load the locks with the cut ends on the tines. I like to spin all fibers from the cut end, because I find that the fibers slide past each other more easily when the scales of the wool are facing backward (toward the tip end) as I draw them out and spin. When I load the fibers with the cut ends on the tines, I know that if I make an odd number of combing passes, I will be pulling from the cut end of the fibers when I begin to draw my top off the comb. Some spinners who comb their fleece don't arrange fibers with tips and butts aligned, and if you aren't worried about that, then you can load the fibers in whatever way is most convenient for you. After you have practiced lashing-on and combing for some time, the lashing-on will become quicker, but as you practice, it is important to lash-on carefully.

For longer-stapled wools, or for a fleece that may be particularly special, it might be a good idea to flick the locks using the tapping method before lashing on. If the locks are open, it makes the combing much easier and can cut down on waste.

Avoiding waste. It's difficult to estimate how much loss results from combing, but you can consider a few things to minimize waste. The cleaner the fleece, the less loss. Similarly, more second cuts result in more waste. If the locks are cotted (matted) in any place, then more loss is to be expected. In general, with a good fleece, I expect to lose about 10 to 15 percent to combs that have been loaded well. If you're a beginner, expect a little more loss at first until you get comfortable with the combing process.

When you use any handcombs, it's important to think safety first. When you follow the combing steps described on the upcoming pages, keep in mind that combs have the potential to hurt if not handled with care and following the correct method.

Combing Is Not Just for the Longwools

Although combing is the best fiber prep choice for the longwools, you don't have to reserve it only for those fleeces. Any fiber that extends past the front tines of your combs can be combed. I generally like a staple length of at least 3 inches for my 2-pitch handcombs, and a bit longer for my English combs. Staple lengths as short as 2 inches can be successfully combed, however, if you use small, fine-toothed handcombs.

STEP-BY-STEP COMBING

STEP 1. When using handheld combs, one comb will do more work than the other as the wool is transferred. Hold the empty comb in your dominant hand. Point the tines of the loaded comb mostly up, but tilted slightly away from your face and body.

Step 1

STEP 2. Make your first combing stroke at the very tips of the fibers, moving the comb perpendicular to the stationary comb and away from your body.

STEP 3. Work gradually in toward the base of the tines, transferring the wool from the loaded comb to the empty comb a bit more with each stroke. When it becomes more difficult to transfer the fibers, I like to give the moving comb a bit of a twist at the end of the stroke to help remove more from the stationary comb. When you've transferred all the fibers you can to the moving comb, you have completed one pass.

STEP 4. Switch hands in a way that is both comfortable and safe. It may take some practice and experimenting to find the best method for you. Another option is to put one of the combs down, then trade places with the comb you are still holding.

For most wools, three passes is sufficient to open the locks, but sometimes it takes four or even five passes. But it's important to make as few passes as possible, as too many can result in neps in finer wools and more tangling and waste in others. When you are finished combing, the fiber on the comb should be completely open, with no obvious locks remaining.

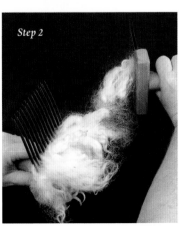

Step 2

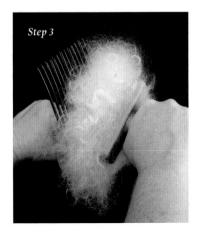

Step 3

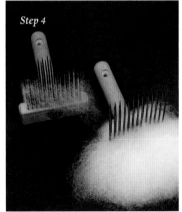

Step 4

Using Dutch and English Combs

The advice about handheld combs I've just given is for using Viking combs. These are the combs I use most often for small projects and sampling. If I were going to be combing an entire fleece, however, or even just enough of a large fleece to make a project like an adult-size sweater, I would use combs with a bit more capacity, such as English or Dutch combs.

STEP-BY-STEP WITH DUTCH COMBS

Dutch combs are 2-pitch combs. Instead of both combs having handles, however, one has a handle and one does not and is always clamped to a table. Dutch-style combs may have longer tines than handheld 2-pitch combs, and so they hold more fiber in each load.

STEP 1. Load the stationary comb lock by lock.

STEP 2. The tines of the stationary Dutch comb are always upright, and so for the first pass, you move the comb from side to side. You can swing it from right to left or left to right, depending on which is most comfortable for you, though you may want to go through the fibers from both sides in order to transfer the most wool onto the moving comb.

STEP 3. Once the fiber has been transferred to the moving comb, take it in a north–south direction to transfer it back to the stationary comb. Keep its tines perpendicular to those of the stationary comb. As with hand-combs, begin at the tips of the fiber farthest from the comb itself and continue to move closer to the stationary comb until the moving comb's tines are sliding next to the wood of the stationary comb, and there's no more wool to transfer.

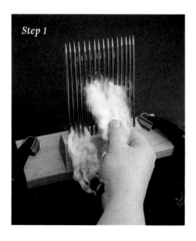
Step 1

Step 2

Step 3

STEP-BY-STEP WITH ENGLISH COMBS

English combs generally have four or five rows of tines, and both combs have a handle. Usually these combs are very heavy, and so clamping one of them to a table and using the other as the moving comb will be more comfortable.

STEP 1. When you lash onto the English combs, the tines should be facing upward. Load the comb lock by lock, using the last ½ inch or so of the staple length. Don't worry about loading it all the way to the last row of the comb. This is different from the way you load a 2-pitch comb, although in both cases you want the staples securely on the comb.

STEP 2. Once the locks are lashed onto the comb, you have two choices for your method of combing. You can keep the tines pointing up and take the moving comb in an east-to-west motion (a), or you can turn the tines to the side and swing the comb from north to south (b), being careful not to hit your leg.

In their books, both Peter Teal (*Hand Woolcombing and Spinning*) and Allen Fannin (*Handspinning Art and Technique*) describe doing one combing pass and then pulling the fiber from the comb, removing any noils and waste, and lashing-on the fiber again. This is a perfect method for hand combing and gives fantastic results, but I don't generally do it this way. I usually just make the three passes, moving the fiber from the stationary comb to the working comb, back to the stationary comb, and one more time back to the working comb. I'm then ready to pull the fibers off into top that is ready to spin. This is definitely a simplified version of what Mr. Teal and Mr. Fannin recommend, but I have been extremely happy with my results.

Step 2a

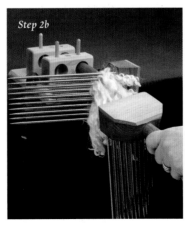

Step 2b

Making Top after Combing

A diz is a tool that helps you remove fiber from a comb and create a nice length of top that is a consistent thickness and ready to spin. Many dizzes have several holes of varying sizes, so that you can choose the size most appropriate for the yarn you intend to spin: a large hole for bulky yarn, a smaller hole for a finer yarn. Although I've used flat items (such as buttons or knitting needle gauges) as a diz in the past, I prefer a curved diz, because the curve serves as a funnel to move all of the fiber ends in the right direction. Here's how to use one.

USING A DIZ

STEP 1. Make a little twist in the end of the fiber before you insert it into the diz. This serves two purposes: It makes it easier to thread the fiber through the hole, and then, when you're ready to spin, it also identifies the cut end of the fiber, which, for me, is the end I want to spin the top from.

STEP 2. Thread the fiber through the hole in the diz, with the curved side facing the fiber.

STEP 3. Push the diz back toward the comb to the point where you begin to feel the tiniest bit of resistance. Don't push it tight into the fiber, as this will make pulling the fiber from the comb almost impossible. Until you get a feel for it, it's better to push the diz back less than you may think is necessary. As you work through this process, keep in mind that if something is too difficult, then you need to adjust the way you're using the diz.

Step 1

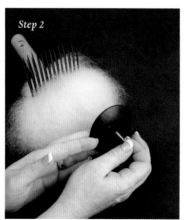

Step 2

Step 3

STEP 4. Pull the fiber out of the comb, through the diz, and toward you (a), then push the diz back toward the comb (b), again just to the point of a little resistance. To avoid thin spots in the top, I try to pull out a little less than one staple length of fiber at a time. Thin spots in your top just beg for drafting troubles during spinning.

STEP 5. Stop pulling fiber when you begin to see noils or waste coming off the comb. The purpose of combing is twofold: One is to align all of the fibers, and the second is to remove all of the short, weak fibers and vegetable matter (VM). Since one of your goals is to separate what you want from what you don't want, you don't need to feel bad about discarding undesirable fiber at this point.

STEP 6. Beginning with the last end of fiber that you drew off the comb, wind the top around your hand, adding a bit of twist with each wrap.

When you get to the end with the point for easy threading you made in step 1, tuck it down in the center of your new little "bird's nest," with the twisted end sticking out. You can store all of these pretty bird's nests in a basket or box until you are ready to spin them.

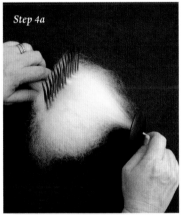

Step 4a

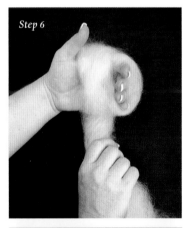

Step 6

Step 4b

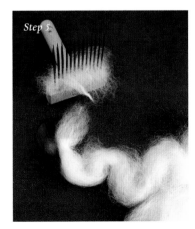

Step 5

done!

MAKING TOP WITHOUT A DIZ

You can follow a similar process of removing the fiber from a comb without using a diz. The yarn that you spin from top taken from the comb in this way, however, will not be as smooth or lustrous as top made with a diz.

STEP 1. Again put a little twist at the beginning as a reminder of which end to start spinning from when it's time to use the prepared fiber.

STEP 2. Pull about one staple length of fiber from the comb. Keep in mind the staple length as you won't have the diz to remind you of how far back to move your hand for the next pull of fiber.

STEP 3. As when you're using a diz, stop pulling fiber when you begin to see noils or waste coming off the comb.

SPINNING FROM THE COMB

I love to spin right off of the comb, because it's one less step. Done this way, the yarn will be fuzzier and fluffier than yarn spun from combed top that has been pulled through a diz, but it is so much fun to spin.

STEP 1. Take the comb that has the last pass of combed fiber on it and hold it in the hand in which you usually hold your fiber supply. Join the fiber on the comb to your leader in whatever way you like best, then start spinning. I like to tip the tines of the comb away from the orifice so that the fiber doesn't work its way up and off the tips of the tines while I'm spinning.

STEP 2. I prefer to use a short forward draw when I spin from the comb, because I feel that it gives me a bit more control over the thickness of the yarn. Just as when you're spinning with the fiber supply in your hand, shorter fibers do better with a woolen-style draft (allowing the twist into the fiber supply) than longer-stapled fibers do. (For more information, see page 122.)

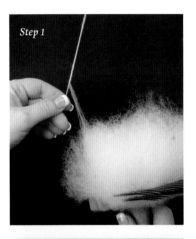

Step 1

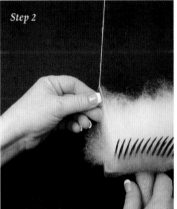

Step 2

A Short Lesson in Worsted Spinning

In a nutshell, a worsted draft is one where the twist is pinched off with your forward hand and not allowed to enter the fiber supply. Most often this is done by using a short forward draw. In a short forward draw, your front hand is pinching the twist to keep it from entering the fiber supply at the same time that it (your front hand) is doing the drafting. I prefer using this method for long-wools in particular, because the result helps to accentu-ate the natural luster in these wools. In addition, it can be more difficult to use a woolen drafting method for wools with a staple length longer than 5 or 6 inches.

SPINNING WORSTED-STYLE WITH A SHORT FORWARD DRAW

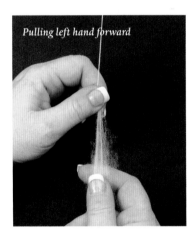

Pulling left hand forward

5 inches in length, I spread my hands about 7½ inches apart. Keep your back hand (the one holding the fiber supply) station-ary. I like to rest my hand or forearm comfortably on my lap or hip, depending on how long the staple length is. Because it can be fatiguing, I don't like to hold the fiber without support, especially for long spinning sessions.

rhythm to it: pull forward, slide back, pull forward, slide back. Each time your fingers slide back to get more fiber, the goal is to grab a similar amount of fiber as the last draft. Your eyes can trick you, so it's important to trust your touch in this situa-tion. Practice will also help you to improve.

STEP 1. As you spin, keep your hands more than a staple length apart; I like at least one-and-a-half staple lengths between my hands. For instance, if I'm spinning Romney, which might be about

STEP 2. With your forward hand about a half staple length toward the orifice, slide your fin-gers back to the tip of the fiber supply to get another bit, keep-ing the twist on the orifice side of your hand. There's kind of a

Tips for Achieving a Perfect Skein

- I like the draft to be about a half staple length, because I find that this gives me the smoothest and most consistent yarns.

- Strive to be consistent with your treadling and twist, and you will be on your way to a perfect skein.

- Change your pinch pressure a bit between the drafting forward and the sliding back.

- If your fingers get sore when spinning like this, try loosening your pinch. You can get away with a lighter pinch than you think possible and still control the twist. If this isn't working, then you may need to turn down the take-up tension on your wheel, which allows you to release a lot of the tension you need in your hands.

SPINNING WORSTED-STYLE WITH A SHORT BACKWARD DRAW

Another way to do a worsted-style draft is called short backward draw, but I find it a little more difficult to achieve a consistent skein when I use this method. The yarn also tends to be a bit fuzzier than yarn spun with a short forward draw. I think the reason for the inconsistency is that you must move your entire arm to draft this way, and this giant movement is difficult to do exactly the same way for each draft. In contrast, a short forward draw requires moving only your hand and wrist. Because you're using a much smaller movement, it's much easier to control the drafting length. In spite of the potential for inconsistency, some fibers seem to like this drafting method, so if you're having difficulty with the short forward draw, you may want to experiment with this type of drafting.

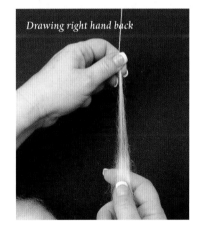

Drawing right hand back

STEP 1. Pinch the fiber supply with the fingers of your forward hand; always keep that hand stationary as you spin.

STEP 2. Draw back your hand that is holding the fiber supply, then move your hand forward, as you allow the newly drafted fibers through the pinch in your forward hand.

WENSLEYDALE

The Wensleydale breed originated in England in 1839. It's one of the few breeds that can be traced to one single progenitor. His name was Bluecap, and he is described as a magnificent ram with the darkest blue skin and the whitest of white wool. The result of a cross of a Dishley Leicester with a Teeswater, he was considered to be the best ram in northern England at the time.

The breed came into the United States only recently (about 1999) through an upgrading program under which semen from a British ram is used to impregnate a ewe from a long-wool breed available in the United States, such as Cotswold, Lincoln, or Leicester Longwool. This results in a lamb that is a 50 percent Wensleydale. This lamb is then crossed with more imported 100 percent Wensleydale semen to get to 75 percent Wensleydale blood. By the fifth generation, the lambs are 96 percent and

considered pure U.S. Wensleydale. (A similar upgrading system is also currently being used in the United States for other longwool breeds, such as Teeswater and Gotland.)

Wensleydales have long, curly locks, but they don't have what is normally described as crimp. The fibers look much like yarn does when it's been knit and then unraveled. This kind of S-shaped crimp is sometimes referred to as *purl,* but I like to call it crimp as it is less confusing, and then everyone understands the reference. Wensleydale fibers generally have between 3 and 5 crimps per inch. This is a hint that the fibers are on the strong, or coarse, end of the micron spectrum. (This conclusion is not definitive, however, as some other wools, such as Dorset Horn or Poll, can have a similar micron count but up to twice the number of crimps per inch.) The fibers range from 30 to 36 microns, which puts Wensleydale firmly on the coarse end of medium fibers. In spite of this, there is something about Wensleydale — that silkiness, that luster — that makes it an attractive wool for garments.

Wensleydale wool grows a staple length of up to 6 inches for a twice-a-year shearing, or a total of 12 inches (sometimes even longer) in a year. A Wensleydale sheep in full fleece is indeed a magnificent sight to behold. The locks are separate and easy to see. With gentle washing, using my small-batch washing methods, rather than washing the whole fleece at one time, they manage to stay together pretty well. There is very little need for containment in netting or bags to maintain the lock structure (see page 68).

Processed Wensleydale top is available everywhere now, in both dyed and natural colors. Although processed Wensleydale is almost always white, you can find raw fleece in colors ranging from white to gray to almost pure black. Some wools seem to be affected more than others by chemical processing. This is true for all longwools, but especially for Wensleydale, although you must also take into account the source of the fiber. Many British longwools are coarser overall than those raised in the United States, and most of the combed top that is generally available comes from large mills and is originally from Great Britain. It might not be quite fair, therefore, to compare a longwool fleece you are handcombing to the combed top you purchased at your local fiber shop.

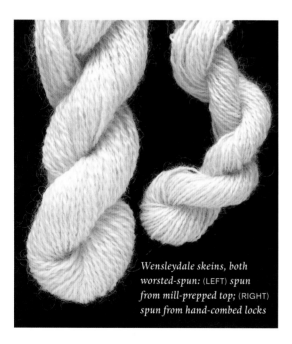

Wensleydale skeins, both worsted-spun: (LEFT) *spun from mill-prepped top;* (RIGHT) *spun from hand-combed locks*

Sampling Wensleydale

I'm not going to lie. Wensleydale has been at the top of my list of wools to spin for the last 10 years. Its luster and silkiness always make me smile. It's not a favorite of some of my spinning friends, and that's okay, but I will always have a special place in my spinning heart for Wensleydale. I combed the wool for these four samples, but after combing, I handled each in a different way.

❶ 3-ply, spun from the fold. For this yarn, I first made top using a diz, and then separated the top into 6- to 8-inch lengths and spun from the fold, allowing twist into the fiber supply. I then plied the singles to make a 3-ply yarn. My goal was to spin a lofty yarn for warmth, which is why I chose to make a 3-ply. It definitely will be warm, but since Wensleydale fleece is already dense and heavy, this yarn is heavier than I'd like. A better choice would be 2-ply, to lessen the overall weight of the finished item, though I usually like a 3-ply for plain knitting. The sample's luster is lovely, but I think this heavyweight yarn might be better used in a woven fabric, which might be considerably lighter than a knitted item.

Spinning this top from the fold with a woolen-style drafting method also caused the yarn to be a little less consistent than I would like. It has a bit of additional twist to make up for the shortened fiber lengths caused by folding them in half. The durable Wensleydale fiber combined with extra twist and a bit thicker yarn makes it great for a high-wear product, such as a bag or purse for daily use.

① — Wensleydale —
combed and dizzed/
woolen-spun 6- to
8-inch lengths from
the fold/
3-ply

❷ **3-ply, spun off the comb.** This yarn is also a 3-ply, but it's much less dense. In this case, I also allowed the twist to go into the fiber supply, but because I spun it right off the comb, the result is completely different from the 3-ply that I spun from the fold (page 127). The yarn is lovely, and the knitted swatch is even better, with great drape, a silky hand, and a slight halo, which I expect will increase over time.

Because of the drape and silkiness of the knitted swatch, I was expecting a little more of the same in my woven sample, but instead I got a bit of a surprise. The luster is beautiful, but the fabric has a lot of body. This would make a great rug or other home-decorating item. I wonder if the hand would change if I changed the sett (ends per inch), or if I didn't beat the warp so closely, even though I tried to use a light hand in the beat. I wove a fairly balanced weave. This woven swatch makes me want to experiment even more with this yarn.

❸ **Fine 3-ply.** For this yarn, I combed the fleece, pulled it from the comb through a diz, and then spun worsted. The 3-ply yarn is about 20 wraps per inch (the number of thicknesses of yarn that can fit in a 1-inch width). The angle of twist here is the same as in sample 2, but it has less twist than sample 1. Usually we say that a fine yarn needs more twist, and so it would follow that this yarn should have more twist than the other two. The reason it is a strong yarn even with less twist is because of its staple length, which is 6 to 7 inches. The longer length needs fewer twists per inch (tpi) to hold the fibers together. If you needed a stronger yarn, for instance for warp, carpeting, or a very hard-wearing knitting yarn, you might want a higher tpi, but to maximize shine, drape, and silkiness, you need a lower tpi. As I recommended earlier (see pages 44–45), using crimps per inch as a starting point for twists per inch is a good rule of thumb to follow. This skein makes that match.

I didn't make a woven sample from this yarn, though this is the yarn I'd shoot for as a weaving yarn.

❹ **Laceweight 2-ply.** This fine yarn is about 80 wraps per inch in thickness. I spun it worsted from fibers pulled from the comb through a diz. The knitted lace swatch I made with it is delicate with beautiful luster. It has a great halo, which will continue to develop as the swatch is handled. This yarn is gossamer fine and comfortable to wear on my neck. It would also make a beautiful weaving yarn. I can imagine it as a shawl with beautiful drape.

2
— *Wensleydale* —
combed/
woolen-spun
from the comb/
3-ply

4
— *Wensleydale* —
combed and dizzed/
worsted-spun/
2-ply/laceweight

3
— *Wensleydale* —
combed and dizzed/
worsted-spun/
3-ply

ROMNEY

Romney sheep were originally known as
Romney Marsh sheep. In the mid-nineteenth
century, Romney Marsh sheep, which had been
adapting to a damp, marshy location for centuries, were modified or improved by crossing
with Dishley Leicesters. The latter breed is now
extinct but is an ancestor of the modern English
Leicester, as well as in the background of many
other modern breeds. As Romneys became
more popular in England, they were known
as the Kent sheep. Between 1900 and 1955,
Romney sheep were exported from England to
43 countries, and they now are found all around
the world, referred to simply as Romneys.

   The fleece of this breed is dense, but the
locks hang separately from each other, as with

These cozy socks were handspun with yarn from Romney top dyed by Hello Yarn; spun and knit by Adrian Bazilla.

making it useful for next-to-skin items, as well as for hard-wearing items like jackets, bags, and even rugs. The crimp structure may not make you first think of longwools, because rather than having the open crimp of a Wensleydale or Lincoln, Romney's crimp is more similar to a wool like Corriedale. The longwool heritage is there in the background of the sheep, however, and shines through in the luster of this wool. Lamb fleeces or some of the finer Romneys may be soft enough for next-to-skin wear, many are great for outerwear and lace, and then there are fleeces at the coarser end of the spectrum that would hold up well to hard wear.

Due to the closer crimp in these fleeces compared to that in most of the other long-wools, there is a bit more natural elasticity in the fibers and yarns from this breed, which makes it even more desirable in both knit-ted and woven clothing. The closer crimp also means Romney yarns will be airier, less dense, and less heavy than those of the other longwools. Romney makes the perfect wool for a lovely lightweight lace shawl, shrug, or sweater. It has less tendency to halo, which makes items made with it less warm than with those that halo more. (Those halos may look innocent enough, but they really do trap warm air.)

Because it's very easy to work with, Romney is a great place to begin when choos-ing your first fleece to tackle and process yourself. The fleece gives about a 70 percent yield after washing, which indicates that it isn't generally very greasy. Although here I describe combing the Romneys, the lock length is not

the other longwools. The locks have a wavy crimp with pointed tips. On the international market, white fleece is preferred, and therefore most Romney sheep are white. Gray, black, and brown fleeces can be found, however, and the American Romney Breeders' Association registry includes colored Romneys. Fleeces can weigh from 8 to 12 pounds, with fiber diam-eter ranging from 29 to 37 microns. The locks average 4 to 8 inches in length, with consistent crimp from butt to tip.

Among the most versatile fleeces I have run into, Romney is one of those breeds with an all-around wool. This fleece is easy to find for spinning in both raw form and processed top. It's also available in a wide range of fiber diameters, so long that it couldn't be flicked, handcarded, drumcarded, or just spun right from the clean lock with no processing. In spite of this, I prefer to comb Romney fleece in order to showcase its beautiful shine.

Sampling Romney

I find when that when I spin Romney, my yarns are more consistent than those of some other breeds with a shorter staple length, and using Romney yarns is always a pleasure. Everything about this breed makes it a favorite of those who try spinning it. And the yarns spun from this wool make it attractive to all textile people.

❶ 3-ply worsted. As mentioned, Romney fleece tends to have a bit less halo than other longwool breeds, no matter whether it has been spun in a woolen or a worsted style. The knitted fabric swatch made with this 3-ply yarn, which was combed, dizzed, and spun worsted with a short forward draw, has a nice smooth finish. The cable is distinct and stands up against the background, giving a nice show of the stitches' structure.

❶ — Romney —
combed and dizzed/
worsted-spun
with a short
forward draw/
3-ply

2 — Romney —
combed/no diz/
woolen-spun 6-
to 7-inch lengths
from the fold/
3-ply

❷ 3-ply spun from the fold. At the opposite end of the spectrum of the purely worsted-spun sample on the previous page is this yarn that is spun from the fold. For this, I pulled the fiber from the comb without a diz. I then took the long strip of fiber and separated it into shorter lengths (6–7 inches) and then spun those lengths from the fold. Though this 3-ply yarn is from the same fleece as the sample spun in a purely worsted manner, it appears to be much lighter and less yellow in color. This is due to the additional air and loft built into the yarn. This loft also results in a bouncier yarn. Knit up, it would be a fabric you would want to pull around you in a chill, whereas the denser construction of the worsted-spun yarn would make a garment that was harder-wearing but not as warm.

The fabric created with the woolen-spun yarn made this way also has a nice halo, giving the stitches a hazy appearance, while the stitches made with the worsted-spun yarn are very clear and distinct. This is something to keep in mind when choosing a spinning technique for colorwork. The worsted-spun yarn gives crisper color changes, whereas the colors will blend somewhat where they intersect when you knit with a more airy yarn.

❸ & ❹ 2-ply worsted. Romney wool is considered to have a *demi-luster,* which means it has some shine but not as much as some of the Leicesters or Teeswater. The way to pick up that shine is by prepping and spinning it using worsted methods, and then making a 2-ply yarn. This approach ensures that as many fibers as possible are facing the light and reflecting it back. This yarn is perfect for knitted lace or fine weaving.

The 2-ply yarn (3) was combed, dizzed, and spun with a worsted draft, so it is a completely worsted yarn. The lower twist gives it a soft feel. The lace I knit with this yarn has a beautiful drape, and it is already beginning to develop a bit of a halo. (The halo in Romney yarns tends to develop less than in some other longwool breeds, but it is there nonetheless.)

I made this woven sample with yarn spun directly from the comb (4). Spinning right from the comb offers a bit of a shortcut compared with using the diz, but the yarns are slightly less consistent than those spun from top. The woven sample has both body and shine. It was roughly finished in hot water and wool wash with hand agitation for about a minute. The sample shrank very little, and the spaces between the threads didn't close as I had hoped. I know that Romney can full and felt, but this varies from fleece to fleece; if this is what you want, it's best to sample the fleece first. It also may be that I should have agitated it for a much longer time.

❸ — Romney —
*combed and dizzed
worsted-spun/
2-ply*

❹ — Romney —
*combed/
worsted-spun
from the comb/
2-ply*

LINCOLN

One of the very oldest longwool breeds, Old-Style Lincoln can be traced back hundreds and some might even say thousands of years. The British shepherd Robert Bakewell is famous for crossing different sheep breeds to modify or improve his flock. He crossed Old-Style Lincolns with some native sheep to develop an old-style Leicester sheep that no longer exists but is the foundation of the English Leicesters we know and love today.

Then called Dishley Leicesters, these sheep were bred back with the Old-Style Lincolns to improve that breed, resulting in the improved Lincolns that are the dual-purpose sheep we are now familiar with. Old-Style Lincolns were described as having a long, weak frame. Compare that with the modern Lincoln sheep, which are arguably the largest-bodied and heaviest-fleeced of all sheep breeds; adults range from 200 to 350 pounds, with fleeces weighing from 11 to 16 pounds. Because of this successful breeding program, these sheep were valued and exported throughout the world to improve breeds in Australia, the United States, New Zealand, and South America.

Until the late 1800s, Lincoln sheep continued to be one of the most popular breeds, but as people sought out sheep with less fatty meat, as well as finer fleeces, the Lincoln fell out of favor, and it is now listed on both British and American endangered sheep lists. This is unfortunate, as the Lincoln has played such a prominent role in the development of so many other useful and popular breeds.

Lincoln fleece cannot be mistaken for wool in any category other than the longwools. Although it's a silky fleece, many people think of it as coarse. It is also generally a very strong wool, but as with so many other breeds, fleeces vary from sheep to sheep, so that you might find one that would make a great cardigan, whereas another would be better for a hard-wearing carpet. The fiber of the eighteenth-century Old-Style Lincolns was coarser than that of the modern Lincoln sheep, and British Lincoln fleeces do seem to be stronger than those of their American cousins, so although the shine and halo are lovely, you might not want to consider making a scarf from a British Lincoln fleece.

Lincolns are both white and colored, and these are on different breed registries through the National Lincoln Sheep Breeders Association in the United States. The lustrous fibers take dye well and give vivid colors; overdyeing a gray fleece gives wonderful jewel tones.

Lincoln locks range from 7 to 15 inches for one year's growth. This length lends itself well to worsted preparation and spinning. With wools of this staple length, the spinner can add less twist and the fibers will still hold together. With fibers of this strength, less twist is key to having the desired drape and hand. Too much twist results in a coarse, ropey yarn; too little twist, in too much pilling. Sampling is key. Follow my suggestions for spinning to the crimp (see pages 44–45), and you'll have better luck when trying to preserve the silky feel of this wool.

Fiber diameters average 33.5 to 44 microns, which is definitely on the strong end of the scale and the upper end for most wools. If the fibers are spun with low twist, the resulting yarns can be soft enough for clothing, but most people would not like to wear them directly next to the skin.

Though Lincoln is not on the top of the list for most spinners, I suggest that everyone try it at least twice and from two different sources before making a final decision about this wonderful and useful wool.

Sampling Lincoln

For this breed I made four different yarns and four knit swatches. Lincoln also makes a very strong weaving yarn for both warp and weft. In order to reduce the halo, if I were going to use this yarn in weaving, I would add more twist. With these longwool breeds, it would be difficult for you to lose the halo completely, but if you add more twist, you can tone it down.

I spun all of the samples here with 3 twists per inch (tpi) to match the 3 crimps per inch in the lock; this is true of both the 2- and 3-ply yarns.

❶ **Worsted-spun bulky.** I spun my first sample exactly as I would expect of a 3 tpi yarn. It is extremely bulky. I combed the fibers, then dizzed them into top and spun with a short forward draw. This knit swatch reminds me of a bulky boyfriend sweater.

❶ — Lincoln —
combed and dizzed/
worsted-spun
with a short
forward draw/
2-ply

❷ 2-ply woolen-spun. I spun this 2-ply yarn a bit finer, but still with 3 tpi. Even though I spun this yarn from the comb with a woolen draft, the luster of the wool really shines through in the knitted swatch due to the combination of spinning a finer yarn and spinning a low twist. The swatch has a bit more drape and also feels silkier than the one knit with the bulkier yarn.

❸ 3-ply woolen-spun. I combed and dizzed the 3-ply yarn, then spun from the fold with a woolen draft. This yarn is much fuzzier than the first two. The luster is hidden, but because of the folded fibers, the yarn has more bounce than the other two, which are bit more compacted. The fold encourages the fibers to press outward to return to their elongated state, and this in turn affects the bounce and squoosh factor of both the yarn and the knitted fabric.

This technique could also be used to produce a loftier woven fabric from wools in the longwools category.

❹ Laceweight Lincoln. Lace yarns are not the thing most spinners think of when considering Lincoln. This fine yarn is about 25 wraps per inch, but it still has only 3 tpi. The halo reminds me of the halo from mohair lace, and this swatch hasn't even had the amount of wear that a lace garment would have. More wear will result in more halo as well as more warmth, because the halo adds to the insulating properties of the piece. The lace is drapey, with a nice weight and a silky hand. Though this yarn does not have the softness of a finer wool, neither does it have a huge prickle factor, because the ends of the fibers are mostly curled under in the halo.

This market bag crocheted with singles yarn made from Lincoln fleece was designed and crocheted by Denny McMillan.

2 — *Lincoln* —
combed/
woolen-spun from
the comb/
2-ply

3 — *Lincoln* —
combed and dizzed/
woolen-spun
from the fold/
3-ply

4 — *Lincoln* —
combed and dizzed/
worsted-spun/
2-ply/laceweight

BLUEFACED LEICESTER

Referred to simply as BFL for short, Bluefaced Leicesters (pronounced LESS-ters) are sometimes called Hexham Leicesters, because they originated near Hexham, England. The rams were originally used to create a mule sheep, and they are still used that way today. A mule sheep is a crossbreed particularly good for meat production. For example, a BFL ram crossed with a Scottish Blackface ewe gives a Scotch mule. But the length, shine, and crimp of the Bluefaced ram comes through, making the fleeces of the mule sheep as desirable for hand-spinning as the pure BFL fleeces.

The Leicesters have a most interesting history, dating all the way back to the Roman occupation of England. As we saw earlier in this chapter, Dishley Leicesters are ancestors of English Leicesters, which in turn were modified by crossings with Teeswater and possibly Cheviot, resulting in Border Leicesters, which

have even finer crimp and finer wool than the English or Leicester Longwools. In the late 1800s and early 1900s, Border Leicesters were being selected for finer fleeces and black skin, and then they were crossed with Wensleydales, which also have black skin under a white fleece. The resulting "blue-faced" sheep were originally used as a crossing sheep with more-coarse hill breeds, and it was found that using rams with darker skin and finer fleece produced a better crossbred ewe. By the mid-1960s, shepherds who were raising these sheep, which were being called "the Great Improvers," formed the Bluefaced Leicester Breeders Association.

Bluefaced Leicesters are categorized as a longwool breed, even though their lock length (3 to 6 inches) and fleece weight (2½ to 4½ pounds) are small compared to some of their cousins. The Bluefaced Leicester has the softest wool of all the longwool breeds. The average fiber diameter is between 24 and 28 microns, with no kemp or hair fibers. You get durability and a similar luster typical of longwool sheep, as well as an affinity to dye. Add to that the bonus of next-to-skin softness, and you can see why Bluefaced Leicester fibers and yarns are extremely popular with the fiber crowd.

The majority of these sheep are white, but you can find colored wool, called black, though it is generally a light grayish brown. The finest of the longwools, BFL is also one of the bounciest and most elastic of this category. It's not as elastic as the high-crimp wools such as Cheviot or Cormo, but due to its tiny ringlets, it has much more bounce than you'll find in a wool, such as Lincoln, with only 1 to 3 crimps per inch.

Most spinners are familiar with the Bluefaced Leicester sold as processed top. The unprocessed fleece can therefore be a bit surprising, with its tiny ringlets and beautiful shine. This is not a fleece I would recommend for a first combing project. The ringlets and long, thin locks make it a bit challenging both to lash onto the combs and also to actually comb. I find that it helps to widen the cut end of the lock a bit and place each lock individually on the comb. This can take a bit more time than you need to give other fleeces in this category, but time taken at the lashing-on stage makes the combing a lot easier and more pleasurable.

As well as the need to be more particular about the way you lash the lock onto the comb, it is extremely important to begin combing at the very tips and work your way back to the comb slowly. I have found that I need to do extra passes with this wool to get all of the fibers opened up and ready for spinning.

Widening the cut end of the lock to place it on the comb

Sampling Bluefaced Leicester

These skeins were a lot of work but so worth it. Even before I plunged them into the hot water for finishing, I found myself holding them to my face and enjoying the feel of them more than once.

1 2-ply worsted. This laceweight skein is truly worsted. I handcombed it, pulled it from the comb using a diz, and spun from the cut end using a short forward draw. I plied the yarn with a very light amount of twist, as my goal was a yarn that would halo and drape nicely as a laceweight yarn. When you examine the yarn closely, you can see that the fibers in it are trying to return to their original state of crimp, and the yarn doesn't lie straight. If I had added enough twist to match the original crimp in the fibers, this would not be happening. Remember to keep your goals in mind when planning a yarn. If I had wanted to enter this skein in competition, it would have been important to have added more twist in the plying step. In addition, if I had wanted less halo, more twist would have helped with that. I used this 2-ply yarn to knit a lace swatch that is quite soft with a lot of drape. It would also make a lovely yarn for weaving.

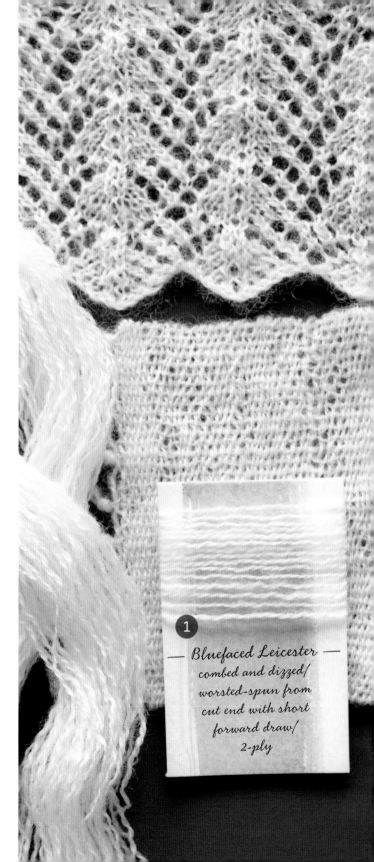

— Bluefaced Leicester —
combed and dizzed/
worsted-spun from
cut end with short
forward draw/
2-ply

❷ 3-ply worsted. I prepared and spun this yarn exactly like the 2-ply version. The 3-ply yarn also has a similar number of twists per inch as the 2-ply (4 tpi), but adding another ply made a big difference in how the yarn behaves. It has a higher luster than the 2-ply and a lot less halo. As you can see by looking at the stockinette swatch, this yarn would make a beautiful lightweight sweater, and because it is next-to-skin soft, it could also be used for an everyday item of clothing.

❸ 2-ply spun from the fold. As with the yarns just described, I combed this fiber and removed it from the comb using a diz. The difference is that I pulled the resulting top into pieces slightly longer than a staple length and spun these pieces from the fold. You can see that this yarn has a great woolen look to it, with its fuzz factor and the luster hiding behind all of those fibers pointing in every direction. The consistency of the skein is very good, however, and the yarn was very easy and quick to spin. I spun the singles a bit thicker than the singles I used for the other two skeins, because my goal for this yarn was warmth. This stockinette-stitch swatch makes me think it would make a good fabric for a mid-January-type sweater for indoors or something to use as outerwear in autumn.

Striped scarf knit with handspun Bluefaced Leicester yarn. I spun the singles on two pairs of bobbins, two for the hand-painted top and two for the undyed top. I then alternated the colors when I plied them to create a continuous yarn with spaced color changes. This gave me stripes with no ends to weave in at each color change.

2

— *Bluefaced Leicester* —
combed and dizzed/
worsted-spun from
cut end with short
forward draw/
3-ply

3

— *Bluefaced Leicester* —
combed and dizzed/
worsted-spun short
lengths from the fold/
2-ply

148

*The socks were knit with yarn
handspun by Adrian Bizilia
with Bluefaced Leicester fiber
dyed by Hello Yarn.*

The Into the Wind shawl was designed by Amy King, and knit with a Bluefaced Leicester/silk blend yarn handspun by Sheril McManaman.

Chapter 6

DOWNS
AND DOWN-TYPE
BREEDS

IN ADDITION TO TRUE DOWNS (Suffolk, Southdown, Oxford, Hampshire, Dorset Down, and Shropshire, for instance), I include in this chapter breeds with wool that looks and acts like that of the true Down breeds. All of the true Downs have colored faces and colored legs, and their wool is usually white. Some have a color gene, but they are the exception to the rule. The locks can be square and blocky or a bit tapered, but they usually are dense. Their fiber diameters run the gamut from the coarse end of Merino to the crisp feel you'd want for yarn intended for a tailored jacket and skirt.

The Down breeds originated in a part of southeast England sometimes called the Downs (meaning "hills"). For years, these breeds have more often than not been referred to as meat sheep, which means that many shepherds and even shearers believe their wool to be worthless. This wool is often sold to a wool pool, a market for fleeces of all breeds of sheep, which are graded, put into large bales, and then auctioned off. (When you buy a garment or a skein of yarn labeled as "wool" with no breed information, chances are there is some Down-type wool in there.) For some shepherds, just getting the wool to the market is a money-losing option, barely covering the shearer's fee, and so instead of trying to sell it, they burn it, use it as mulch, or sometimes just store it. You may be able to find Down-type fleece if you go right to a farm that raises these sheep, but otherwise you may find it difficult to find as spinning fiber, because the unfortunate label "meat breed" has influenced the attitude of many handspinners and shepherds alike who think the wool is not good for yarn and fabric making. Nothing could be further from the truth. These are some of the bounciest and hardest-wearing wools, as well as fun to spin.

The crimp in these wools is remarkable. When you take a whole lock in your hand and look at it, you often can detect very little or no visible crimp structure. The fibers look a bit disorganized. But take out one single fiber and what do you see? Great crimp. Spiral in structure, around and around it goes. The fabulous thing is that crimp has exciting implications for what you can do with the yarns. Its bounciness and resiliency means no more sagging elbows in your sweater and no more stretched-out socks that slide around. In addition, many of these fleeces are very felt resistant. It's true! These are the naturally superwash wools, no chemical processing necessary to avoid felting. Although it hasn't been proven, I believe that this is another beneficial effect of the crimp structure. Because the spiral-shaped crimps constantly push away from one another, they remain independent of their neighbors, rather than lying close to them and moving against each other during washing. I like to think of it this way: Because of their crimp, fibers from other wools fit together like puzzle pieces, whereas the Downs' fibers are puzzle pieces that don't really quite fit. Their spiral crimp also provides great insulation. All of that air between the fibers keeps us warmer in our Southdown sweater than we might be in a sweater knit with yarn spun from one of the longwools.

The micron count places these wools firmly in the middle range of fiber diameters, adding to their strength and wearability and making them appropriate for a wide variety of projects. Though I knew this wool was desirable, it wasn't until I began to prep and spin a wide variety of sample yarns that I realized how truly versatile and useful the Down-type wools could be. Because of the fibers' springiness, durability, and resistance to felting, socks were always my first idea for what to do with

them, but I've come to realize that their value goes well beyond socks. What a great sweater yarn the wool would make, with both resilience and also natural insulating properties!

Not only are these wools very useful, but they are a real pleasure to spin and work with. Some of these fleeces have a longer staple than others, so when you're shopping for any of the Down-type breeds, look for fleeces that are a bit longer stapled. This, of course, will depend on the breed you choose, just as within the other wool categories. Southdown, for instance, ranges from 1½ to 4 inches for a full year's growth; Horned or Poll Dorset may have up to 5 inches growth in a year. Since the sheep are being raised for market, they are often shorn only once a year. Sheep breeds like Wensleydale that have more wool growth — up to 12 inches in a year — are often shorn twice a year, because a 5- or 6-inch staple is much easier for handspinners to manage. On the other hand, if they're being used for show, the Downs may be sheared multiple times a year in order to reveal their body conformation. In this case, the sheep are rarely seen in full fleece, as is true for breeds being raised mainly for their wool.

A word of advice about spinning these fibers: spin the singles finer than you think is necessary for the yarn you want, because the yarns will expand and fluff up when you wash them.

Characteristics of the THE DOWN TYPES

Black Welsh Mountain

Origin: Welsh Mountain
Fleece weight: 2½–5½ lbs.
Staple length: 2"–4"
Fiber diameter: 28–36 microns
Lock characteristics: Dense, blocky; may have some kemp
Color: Black

Clun Forest

Origin: Several British hill breeds
Fleece weight: 4½–9 lbs.
Staple length: 2½"–5"
Fiber diameter: 25–33 microns
Lock characteristics: Crimp varies from sheep to sheep; is not consistent over the lock
Color: White

Dorset Horn/ Dorset Poll

Origin: Spanish Merinos/native Welsh Sheep
Fleece weight: 4½–9 lbs.
Staple length: 2½"–5"
Fiber diameter: 26–33 microns
Lock characteristics: Dense/blocky; irregular crimp
Color: Usually white

Hampshire

Origin: Native Hampshire/ Southdown/Cotswold
Fleece weight: 4½–10 lbs.
Staple length: 2"–4"
Fiber diameter: 24–33 microns
Lock characteristics: Blocky, dense
Color: Usually white

Montadale

Origin: Columbia/Cheviot
Fleece weight: 7–12 lbs.
Staple length: 3"–5"
Fiber diameter: 25–32 microns
Lock characteristics: Dense, uniform crimp
Color: Usually white, but some black

Oxford

Origin: Native sheep/Hampshire/ Southdown/Cotswold
Fleece weight: 6½–12 lbs.
Staple length: 3"–5"
Fiber diameter: 25–37 microns
Lock characteristics: Blocky, dense
Color: White

Shropshire

Origin: Native sheep/Southdown/ Leicester/Cotswold
Fleece weight: 4½–10 lbs.
Staple length: 2½"–4"
Fiber diameter: 24–33 microns
Lock characteristics: Dense, blocky
Color: White (rarely there may be color)

Southdown

Origin: The first Down breed
Fleece weight: 5–8 lbs.
Staple length: 1½"–4"
Fiber diameter: 23–31 microns
Lock characteristics: Dense, blocky
Color: Usually white, some colored

Suffolk

Origin: Southdown/Old-Style Norfolk Horn
Fleece weight: 4–8 lbs.
Staple length: 2"–3½"
Fiber diameter: 25–33 microns
Lock characteristics: Dense, blocky
Color: Usually white, rarely gray

Skirting a Fleece

Often when a farm is raising sheep for meat rather than wool, as in the case of the Down-type breeds, little or no thought is put into the fleece. You may find that the fleeces haven't been skirted (tags and belly wool removed, along with the wool that sees the most wear while it's still on the sheep), and also that there will be some vegetable matter (VM) as well as plenty of dirt. This may look really bad, but usually you can remove the dirt with a few good soaks (see Scouring Down-Type Wools, on this page).

If a fleece you select hasn't been skirted, this process is easy enough to do. Find a place where you can spread the fleece out. When I've helped during shearing at local farms, they usually do this on a skirting table. The table is a wooden frame covered in wide-mesh screening, so that when the fleece is shaken, the larger bits of VM fall to the ground. Most of us don't skirt enough fleeces to make it necessary to obtain a table, so laying out a sheet or other covering is quite adequate for the purpose.

When you spread out the fleece, you'll see that it does want to stay together, so it's easy to spread it out into the shape it was on the sheep. Once you've laid it out, start skirting by just removing the edge bits. You can be brutal about this. Look at it with a critical eye. Are those extremely short fibers going to add beauty to your yarn? Do you really want to try removing that stuff that looks like thick mud, but may not be? That neck wool looks soft, but it will take a ton of time to pick out all of that

VM. Take all that wool that you've removed and put it in your garden. The sheep residue will help to fertilize your plants, and it breaks down so slowly that it will help keep the weeds down. (See page 10 for a photo of an unrolled fleece.)

Scouring Down-Type Wools

The technique for washing the Down-type wools is the same as what is described for the longwools: a wool scour (I use Unicorn Power Scour) and plenty of water with two washes and two or three rinses (see pages 11–12). Many of these breeds have a fairly low grease content, but as I've said, if raised for meat, the fleece may be much dirtier than a fleece from a sheep raised with the handspinner in mind. It therefore takes the same amount of washing and rinsing as does a greasy fleece, but take care not to overscour, as this wool tends to get a little crunchy feeling after being washed. Using a lower temperature in the second wash and all the rinses sometimes keeps the fiber from feeling dry; the hot water is necessary for cutting the grease, but the dirt will come away in cooler water. In previous washing sections, I said to avoid moving the fleece from a hot-temperature bath to a cooler bath. One of the great things about the Down types is that most of them are felting resistant, and so this temperature change won't matter here. (You may want to experiment to confirm that there's no tendency to felt before doing this with a whole fleece.) You can also use a smaller amount of detergent than you would for washing a greasier breed. I sometimes like to put a little Unicorn Fibre Rinse in the last rinse water to counteract the dryness problem. It makes the fibers feel a bit softer, and it also cuts down on static. Some spinners use hair conditioner or cream rinse instead of Fibre Rinse. I avoid conditioners made for human hair as they may contain additives that you may not want on your wool, such as plastics that are difficult to wash away with the gentle washing we use for our wool textiles.

To help judge whether to use a fiber rinse in the last rinse water, wash just a small amount of fiber (an ounce or so) the way you plan to wash the whole fleece. Make sure you let your sample dry completely before making any final decisions. When you hold the scoured sample in your hand, you will know whether to use additives. Once again, experimentation is definitely your friend.

Handcarding Techniques

As I observed earlier, the crimp on most of the breeds in the Down-type category is somewhat spiral shaped. Each fiber likes to be independent and on its own. Instead of being all lined up like soldiers, these fibers want to act like it's a party all the time, resulting in both a possible resistance to felting and that superior insulation that I've been praising. Carding, followed by woolen-type spinning, is fantastic for this

kind of wool, as these techniques show off the Downs' inherent strengths to the greatest advantage. The spiral crimp and elasticity of the fibers react beautifully when spun from a rolag (see page 159), which also encourages the fibers to push out against each other to make that warmest of yarns. I think of all of this as continuing the party.

Because the fiber party's always going on, however, you may find that yarns spun from handcarded fiber are a bit uneven and inconsistent. If you comb wool, you can separate and remove short fibers. This is even true for one of the flicking methods, but it doesn't happen when you card. One of the reasons I prefer carding the Down types rather than combing is the very fact that, because of the short staple length of the fibers, combing results in more waste than I like. Carding these wools results in a blend of fibers of different lengths and strengths, even though it also causes some unevenness and inconsistency in the spun yarn.

You can deal with the inconsistent singles that naturally occur when spinning carded, short-stapled fibers in at least two different ways. The first is to ply more than two singles together. For instance, 3- or 4-ply yarns disguise any number of flaws in the singles. The second is not to worry too much about it. Some of these inconsistencies will work themselves out with proper finishing of the skein, and once the yarn is used to make fabric, many of those issues won't show.

There's one final comment on the advantages of carding over combing or flicking the Down types. While it's possible to use a flicker on some of the longer-stapled ones, it's less advisable for fleeces from breeds like Southdown, which have a naturally short staple length (sometimes less than 3 inches). Getting a good grip on such a short fiber mass may make flicking an unpleasant operation. Your fingers can easily get in the way and be injured.

Picky, Picky

In contrast to combing or flicking, handcarding removes very little VM and none of the second cuts. It is therefore very important to pick out as many large bits of both by hand before you begin the carding process.

Spinners have developed many techniques in the use of handcards. I cover my favorite methods here, but they may not be comfortable for everyone. As you practice, you're likely to find a style that is most comfortable for you. It may be a little challenging to learn to card by following static photos in a book. I encourage you to find someone who cards on a regular basis and ask them to show you, or take a lesson at a nearby fiber festival or shop that sells spinning equipment. Just five minutes with someone demonstrating in person can save you lots of time, struggle, and grief.

You can use flat- or curved-back-style handcards. Spinners usually choose one based on who taught them to card as well as what feels comfortable to them. (For a description of different kinds of handcards, see page 17.) I prefer curved-back handcards because the method for using them is most comfortable for me.

In addition to curved and flat backs, you can select from a number of different carding cloths. The most widely available ones have 72-, 112-, or 212-pins (or teeth) per square inch (you may also see this specified as tpi, or teeth per inch). Cards with a larger number of pins per square inch are the best choice for fine fibers. This doesn't mean that you can't card fine fibers, such as Targhee, on a set of handcards with 72 pins per inch, but you usually need to make more passes to get the fibers completely opened up and ready to spin. More passes means more time spent in fiber prep, and it also means that there is more chance for adding neps to the carded fiber. Sometimes, each end of a fiber stays attached to each card as you transfer the wool from one card to the other. When this happens, the fiber gets stretched and then bounces back, forming a little knot, or nep. To avoid the neps, you need to take more care as you card, including making fewer passes.

No matter which kind of carder you use, don't overload it. When you place your hand on top of the loaded card, you should easily be able to feel the pins through the fiber. Too much fiber makes carding more difficult and harder to manage, and results in more passes to get all the fiber carded. As has been repeated with advice for every preparation method, less is definitely more in fiber prep.

MY FAVORITE METHOD WITH CURVED-BACK HANDCARDS

STEP 1. Take a small handful of fiber and place it about one-third the card's width away from the handle side of the carding cloth. Continue loading small handfuls of fiber across the width of the carder.

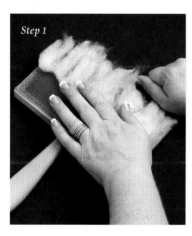

Step 1

STEP 2. Hold the empty carder in your dominant hand and the loaded carder in your other hand, grasping the handle close to the bed of the carder. You can stabilize it with your first and middle fingers. Bring the empty card down to meet the tips of the fibers sticking out from the edge of the loaded card until the pins grab some of the fibers. Flip the empty card up at a 90-degree angle and

pull slightly upward, transferring a portion of the fiber from the card you loaded to the working card.

Step 2

STEP 3. Bring the card to the fiber again, this time placing it slightly closer to the back edge of the loaded handcard, and repeat the motion of step 2.

Step 3

STEP 4. Continue to work the top card over the loaded card, moving gradually closer to the back edge and flipping to a 90-degree angle until you have moved all of the fiber from the bottom card to the top card.

Step 4

STEP 5. At this point, you can switch hands if you like, or you can repeat the same movement in reverse, using the bottom card to grab the fibers from the upper card.

USING FLAT-BACKED CARDS

STEP 1. When you use a flat-backed carder, your motion with the top card (the one you're transferring the fiber to) should be more of a smooth drag, rather than a flip. Although you should avoid grinding the carding pins together, you will hear a bit of a scraping as you go through the transfer process. Only about half the fiber will be transferred with this method.

Step 1

STEP 2. When half the fibers are moved to the originally empty card, a process called *stripping* is used to move the remaining fibers.

Step 2

STEP 3. To strip the fibers from one card to the other, place the front of the card to be stripped against the pins on the handle side of the card that is to receive the fibers (a). Next, move the card being stripped in a downward motion, placing the web of fibers onto the newly charged card (b).

Card the fibers again and then strip the opposite card. You can also use this method on curved-back cards, if desired.

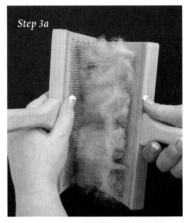

Step 3a

Step 3b

HOW TO MAKE A TRADITIONAL ROLAG

After you've opened up the fibers with your handcards, you can remove the fiber for spinning. The most customary end product of handcarding is when the fibers are rolled from end to end to form what is known as a *rolag*. To get a true woolen yarn, prepare a traditional rolag in this way. The cylindrical shape of the rolag causes the fibers to remain in a somewhat circular pattern as the twist enters the fiber supply. The yarn you prepare and spin this way will have the best insulating qualities of yarns spun by any of the other methods described here.

STEP 1. Position the carder with the handle toward your body. Starting with the ends that hang off the edge of the carder, roll the fibers toward the body of the card and continue to roll them as you remove fibers from the pins little by little. You can do this with your fingers, the edge of your hand, or the edge of the other handcard.

STEP 2. If you have curved-back cards, you can lay the newly formed rolag on the back of one of the cards and roll it between the two cards to compact the fibers and help them stick together. Lay the finished rolags in a basket or other container until you are ready to spin them.

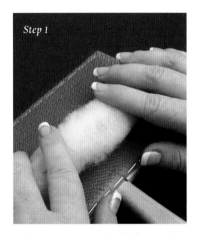
Step 1

Step 2

The Fiber-Cigar Option

If you prefer to preserve fiber alignment, instead of the true woolen-yarn qualities that you get by spinning rolags, you can form what is known as a fiber cigar. With the cigar shape, you can spin a yarn that is a bit smoother than one spun from a rolag, because you are spinning from the tips and butts of the fibers, rather than from the cylindrical rolag.

To create the cigar, remove the small carded batt from the pins of the card and roll it starting at one side edge so that the fibers are lengthwise and parallel on the "cigar," to create a very short package that is fattest in the middle. If you wish, you can draw it out somewhat to make it a consistent thickness that is easier to spin from.

HOW TO SPIN OFF THE CARD

If you are carding fibers that are a bit short for combs but you really want to preserve their alignment, spinning off the card may be the answer. This technique mimics the effect you get by flicking and then spinning from the lock. Because you are allowing short lengths to remain in the fiber bundle, along with any neps or noils contained in the wool, yarn spun using this method doesn't resemble the organized, smooth yarn you get from combing, but it's a good second choice.

STEP 1. Hold the carded, still-loaded handcard with the front edge facing the orifice of your spinning wheel, and attach the fibers from one end of the card to a leader.

STEP 2. Begin to spin, working your way along the front edge of the card until most of the fibers have been removed. Some fibers will remain in the bed of the card and may not have been spun. Don't clean those fibers from the bed; just reload the card and handcard as usual for the next batch. These fibers will be carded in and join the next group to be spun.

Step 1

Step 2

HOW TO MAKE YOUR OWN ROVING

This is a great way to blend different fibers and different colors, as well as make longer lengths of fiber to spin. I like the way it allows me to blend several colors together to achieve a sort of striation or long stripes of several colors together along the length of the roving. For a consistent roving, weigh the first set of batts, and then load the handcards with the same amount of fiber for each subsequent set of batts.

STEP 1. Card your fibers as described for either curved-back or flat-back carders (see pages 157–58). Remove the batt from the bed of the hand-card, keeping it flat (don't form a rolag or cigar). Lay it aside.

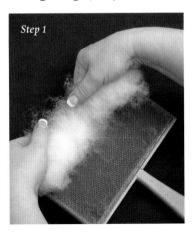

Step 1

STEP 2. Make five to seven of these batts, and stack them one on top of the other. (Five or six batts are comfortable for me to hold, but spinners with larger hands may be able to manage more.)

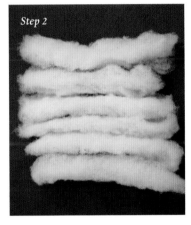

Step 2

STEP 3. Holding the rectangular stack in your hand, begin to draw out fiber from the side (perpendicular to the length of the fibers). Whether you are blending colors or fibers, try to balance the amount of each color or type of fleece as you draw the fibers out. To ensure that you'll have plenty of air and control when you spin from your roving, take care to keep your roving a pretty consistent thickness, generally no thinner than

2 inches thick. Make a second pass, if necessary, to even out what you've made or if you want it to be thinner.

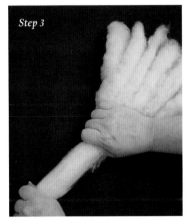

Step 3

STEP 4. Spin the roving as you complete it, or wind it into a loose "bird's nest," adding a little twist to the fiber as you wind to help keep the fibers in place, and put it aside to spin later.

Step 4

Drumcarders

Although I didn't make any of the samples in this book from fleece processed in a drumcarder, it is an excellent option for any spinner who likes spinning from carded fibers. It's not necessarily a faster option. With practice, using handcards can be just as fast as using a drumcarder. Once you develop some drumcarding skills, however, there's nothing much prettier than a beautifully smooth batt fresh off a drumcarder.

You can use the drumcarded fibers in much the same way you work with those from handcards. The drumcarder aligns the fibers as you feed them in, and then you can remove the drumcarded batt in several different ways to get different end results in your yarns: fine or bulky, cool or insulating, and thin or fat.

Less Is Better. A secret to properly done drumcarding is that more is not better. This secret also applies to every other wool-processing method: More on handcards, more on combs, more in the hand for flicking, or more on the drum does not result in faster processing. Please learn from my mistakes! I confess to still getting drawn into thinking I can get just one more layer on that drum. If I give in to this temptation, however, what always happens in the end is that I need to make additional passes no matter what tool I am using, and additional passes just slow me down.

Dos and Don'ts of Drumcarding

- Feed only small amounts of fiber at a time. Too much fiber will get caught between the licker-in and the main drum and make it difficult, if not impossible, to turn the handle. It also encourages the incoming fibers to wrap around the licker-in, resulting in more waste than necessary.

- Turn the handle slowly as you feed in the fibers. Turning the handle too fast, especially when you're working with fine fibers, causes neps to form in the developing batt. This is because one end of the fiber is attached to the main drum while the other is attached to the licker-in. When you turn the handle fast, you cause the fiber to snap, and the spring in the crimp causes it to ball up.

- Do not hold back on the fibers as you feed them in. It's okay to hold them lightly for a bit of control, but let them feed as they like. This helps limit the amount of fiber that wraps around the licker-in. It also helps avoid stretching the fibers, and thus cuts down on neps that can develop during the process.

- If you see fibers beginning to wrap onto the licker-in, use your fingers or a nail brush to sweep those fibers up and onto the main drum. This, too, cuts down on fiber waste.

USING A DRUMCARDER

Preparation is key to good results. By this I mean that you should never just take some washed fleece and throw it at the carder and expect a good output.

STEP 1. Open up all the locks using a flick or a comb. You can also use a *teasing tool,* a device that is covered with carding cloth and comes with some drumcarders. To use it, clamp the tool to a table, and then draw the locks through the pins to open them up. No matter what tool you use, take care to completely open both tips and butts of the locks so they are no longer matted or stuck together. For more tips on getting good results with a drumcarder, see Dos and Don'ts of Drumcarding on the facing page.

Step 1

STEP 2. Put your fiber through the carder in small amounts at a time. You should be able to see the tray of the carder through the fiber you are putting on.

Step 2

STEP 3. Stop adding fiber just before the fiber fills the carding cloth teeth. Keep in mind that less is better and will result in smoother batts.

Step 3

STEP 4. Remove the batt from the carder. Separate the batt by running the batt pick (also called a *doffer pin*) under the fiber along the slot in the large drum. Gathering together the fiber coming from the back of the drum in your hand, pull the batt from the drum. The batt should come off following the direction the carding cloth pins bend.

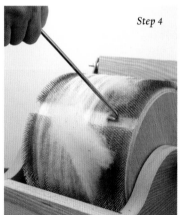

Step 4

STEP 5. If necessary, separate the batt into several lengths and repeat steps 2 through 4 until the fibers are all open, or are as blended as you desire.

PREPARING TO SPIN DRUMCARDED FIBERS

Once you have your drumcarded batt, you have several options to prepare it for spinning. Each method affects the yarn you spin from it, so it's important to sample to make sure you can get the yarn you want.

Option 1. For an effect similar to what you get from a handcarded rolag, just roll the drumcarded batt crosswise, and attenuate it into something similar to an extra-long rolag. The difference between a rolled drumcarded batt and a handcarded rolag is that the fibers are drawn out and thus are more parallel in the drumcarded batt, and the yarn will therefore have a bit less of a woolen look.

Option 2. Roll the batt so the fibers are lengthwise, and then attenuate it as you did for handcarded roving (see page 161).

Option 3. Split the batt lengthwise into several parallel, long strips.

Option 4. Strip the batt in a zigzag fashion to make one long strip of roving.

Option 5. Make a roving right off the drumcarder by using a diz. Here's how: Instead of removing the finished batt in one piece, lift just a small width (an inch or less) from the drum, and thread it through a hole on your diz. Pull the fiber off the drum through the diz little by little, sliding the diz back in increments to keep the width consistent. With this technique, you remove the batt all in one piece and end up with a long strip of roving ready to spin.

SUFFOLK

Suffolk sheep were developed in the 1700s and recognized as a breed by 1810. Their heritage is Southdown crossed with the Old-Style Norfolk Horn. The outcome of this long-ago crossing is a fast-growing sheep that is great for market lamb production. The Suffolk breed didn't land in the eastern United States until 1888 and didn't see the western side of the country until 1919. Today, however, it is the most common sheep breed in North America.

Like the fleece from most of the other Downs and Down-type sheep, Suffolk wool has been overlooked, and available fleeces are generally very dirty, with tons of VM. If you happen upon a shepherd who's interested in wool production, grab one of these fleeces to cut down on your work, because the chances are good that there will be less VM in it than in the fleeces of sheep raised only for meat. If you want to try Suffolk no matter what, go ahead.

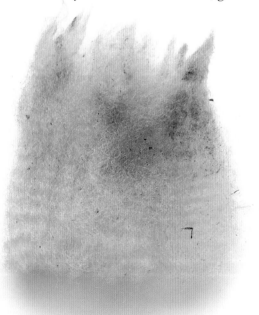

The yarns from this breed are bouncy, airy, and lightweight, while maintaining warmth and durability.

Suffolks are not small sheep; they rival Lincolns in size and weight. Mature rams weigh anywhere from 250 to 350 pounds; ewe weights vary from 180 to 250 pounds. The fleece from a mature ewe weighs between 4 and 8 pounds, with a yield of 50 to 62 percent after skirting and scouring.

The fiber diameter of a Suffolk is between 25 and 33 microns. The staple length ranges from 2 to 3½ inches. These shorter-stapled fibers ask for a bit more twist to hold them together, in order to ensure less pilling and longer wear. The problem is that too much twist equals a harsh yarn. Sampling is your friend once again. Use different spinning techniques to make a few swatches to help you get where you want to go with a lot less wasted time and fiber.

Sampling Suffolk

Suffolk is a surprise to many spinners who expect a harsh hand in this wool, but then discover it is quite often the opposite. Though these yarns wouldn't necessarily be thought of as soft, I wouldn't hesitate to use these sturdy-feeling yarns for a jacket or cardigan that I'd wear next to my neck.

❶ & ❷ **2- and 3-ply woolen-spun.** I spun both the 2-ply and the 3-ply woolen-spun yarns from rolags. These yarns are both stretchy and cushiony. The 3-ply (2) is definitely firmer than the other, and the yarn I used for the knit swatch would make a great cardigan that would last for years. The 2-ply yarn (1) for the other knit swatch is finer and would make a nice warm garment without adding much bulk. I used the same 2-ply yarn for the woven swatch, which has a good amount of body. Yardage made of this yarn would work for a very warm jacket with a collar that stays in place. While it might not make that scarf with great drape that you dream of, it has excellent insulating properties and would guard against the cold.

1
— *Suffolk* —
handcarded/
woolen-spun from
rolags/
2-ply

2
— *Suffolk* —
handcarded/
woolen-spun from
rolags/
3-ply

Worsted-spun. After spinning the purely woolen yarns, I was quite happy with the way they felt and looked. I then carded some more of the Suffolk fiber into rolags, which I spun using a worsted drafting method. Though this yarn is attractive, it feels quite a bit firmer and much less elastic, even though I was careful to avoid adding more twist than I put into the woolen-spun samples.

❸ Laceweight. Lace is not the thing I think of when choosing Down-type wools for spinning. This lace sample is in some ways surprising, and in other ways it did exactly what I imagined. The surprise is that the lace is more open than I expected; because of the bounciness of the yarn, I thought the holes would want to collapse on themselves. The fabric has a lot of body, and so if you are looking for a lace fabric that maintains shape, rather than offering drape, when used in a garment, this might be the best fiber choice. The yarn is somewhat firm, but it is not scratchy.

My Suffolk samples show me exactly what I'd like to use these yarns for and where they will work best. For instance, a worsted-spun sample might do very well if it were spun from the end of the card, rather than from a rolag. I'd also like to experiment more with twist: Should I use less or more twist in a finer 3-ply yarn to achieve the perfect recipe for socks? I'm imagining how I would spin Suffolk yarn for a fine-woven fabric for an A-line skirt that would be extremely warm and comfortable for winter. Also, combing Suffolk makes a beautiful yarn. How might I use that? A study of Suffolk alone could take months and months before I would exhaust all of the prep, spinning, and fabric options. With all of these possibilities, if you are hesitant to try out Downs and Down-type breeds, Suffolk might be a great place to get your feet wet.

3

— Suffolk —
handcarded/
worsted-spun
from rolags/
2-ply/laceweight

Why Not *Suffolk Yarn for Lace?*

Several characteristics of Down-type yarns argue against using them for lace: Thicker spots in these yarns seem to be amplified after washing, probably due to the fantastic, spiral-shaped crimp structure, which causes the fibers to push away from each other. If the twist isn't consistent or the draft was longer or shorter in one spot, it will be obvious after you wash the yarn. In addition, drape is not the strong point of Suffolk yarns, and drape is something we generally look for in lace. Because you have so many options in other wools, I would avoid knitting lace with Down-type fleece for that reason alone.

On the other hand, it's critical that the lace pattern be obvious in the knitted fabric. There is nothing more disappointing than spending a lot of time on a project only to discover that the structure and pattern you worked in, regardless of whether you are knitting, crocheting, or weaving or working some other fiber project, disappears because of the structure of the yarn you used. For a lace project that calls for more stability and structure, this wool might be a great choice.

SOUTHDOWN

You could fill an entire book with all there is to say about the breed history and usefulness of Southdown sheep. Southdowns are the progenitors of all the other Down breeds. The original Southdowns were small bodied and raised for both wool and meat. Records from medieval times include descriptions of sheep that resemble these old-style Southdowns. These small sheep were crossed and selected to develop a larger, more marketable sheep, which is the standard Southdown sheep we see today. The smaller sheep that are much like the original Southdowns are called Babydoll Southdowns or Olde English Southdowns; an even smaller sheep, the Miniature Southdown, is less than 24 inches tall. Babydoll and Miniature Southdowns are currently raised as pets as well as for wool.

Records indicate that Southdown sheep were first brought to the United States from England in 1640 with the Puritan migration, and they were again imported in the early 1800s. Southdown fleeces can now be a bit difficult to find in the United States, however, as other, larger breeds have become more marketable and profitable than even standard Southdowns. The breed has been on the conservancy list of The Livestock Conservancy for some time but has been upgraded to a recovering breed as of 2012. This is great news because, if things continue in this direction, it won't have to be on the list at all.

The wool of Southdown sheep is short, ranging from 1½ to 4 inches, with most locks in the 2- to 3-inch range. Fiber diameter ranges from 23 to 31 microns. The fleeces are soft and bouncy with lots of crimp and loft. Because the fibers are so short, you may experience a lot of loss if you comb them, and the fibers may be difficult to flick. Carding is usually the best bet for these fibers.

When you look for a Southdown fleece, look for one low in VM and with few second cuts. Because you'll be carding this wool, any second cuts and VM will get blended into the fleece when you card. I carded the wool for all of the samples on page 175; although I attempted to remove the second cuts before carding, I was unsuccessful at removing all of them, and so the yarns spun from my carded rolags are extremely textured.

Sampling Southdown

I should point out that not all Southdown should be judged by the samples shown here. Several times while I was spinning my samples for this section, I was tempted to abandon them and search for a different fleece. The fleece I chose had an abundance of second cuts and a staple length of 2 inches or less over the entire fleece. Before washing, the lock length was about 2½ inches, but the fineness of the fibers caused it to shrink a little when scoured. This wasn't due to any felting; it was just that, as the grease and dirt fell away, the fibers were released to do as they wished.

I persevered, however, and decided to go ahead with my samples, because I wanted to show that even not-so-nice fleece can be used for wonderful, utilitarian clothing. I also wanted to include yarns that aren't so great to demonstrate that sometimes, no matter what your skill level, the fiber dictates the final yarn, and no matter what you do, it will not become a smooth, consistent thread. If the project calls for smoothness and consistency, look for a different fleece, and dedicate the unruly one to a project that will work with that yarn. And don't give up on one bad experience with a particular breed, because one fleece may not be a good representative of the entire breed. I've spun wonderful Southdown that is fabulous and has done everything I've wanted it to.

❶ 3-ply woolen-spun from rolags. I spun the yarn from handcarded rolags, then plied it to 3-ply. It has a nice amount of elasticity, and the 3 plies help to even out the singles. Although the plied yarn contains some of the texture that was in the original singles, this gives the swatch a rustic look that can be attractive in some projects. Though medium to soft in feel, the hand of the fabric isn't prickly, and it feels as if it would stand up to lots of use. Because of the short fiber lengths, some pills began to form with about a minute of abrasion.

❷ 2-ply woolen-spun from rolags. Sample 2 is a 2-ply yarn, made from the same singles as sample 1. This yarn, too, has a nice amount of springiness, and the knitted swatch is a bit more supple than the one worked with sample 1. The fabric seems perfect for a sweater, as it feels a little less dense than the 3-ply swatch, though I know that this yarn will pill even more readily than the other, because 2-ply yarns lock in fewer of those ends that stick out and become the pills we see on our clothing.

❸ 2-ply worsted-spun off the card. For the knitted lace swatch, I spun off the card with a worsted-style draft. Although the yarn is a bit smoother than the ones I spun from rolags, the second cuts and short fiber length still contributed to texture and lumps along the length of the yarn. But spinning off the card helped reduce the number of second cuts finding their way into my yarn, since most of them stayed in the pins of the card. I spun the singles somewhat finely, at about 20 wraps per inch, but after plying, the yarn plumped up and the crimp went back into place and the final yarn became much thicker. This is not a yarn I would generally choose for a lace project, since its inconsistencies are even more visible near the empty spaces in the lace, but I can see how this might be a good choice for a heavier shawl with a more unpolished look. It's a matter of fitting the yarn to the right project.

Minimizing Neps

The problems caused by second cuts in these short Southdown fibers can be exacerbated by their fineness and springy crimp, which can result in a lot of neps in the rolag if the fibers are overcarded. With fibers this fine and springy, I try to keep my carding down to one or two passes.

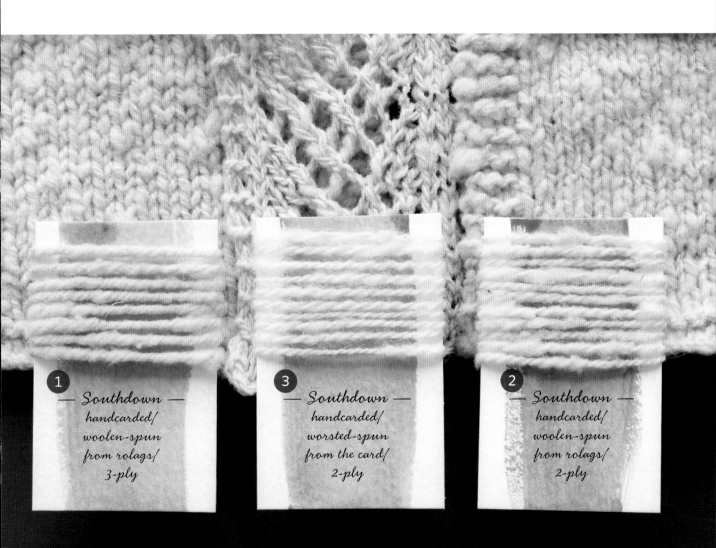

1 — Southdown — handcarded/ woolen-spun from rolags/ 3-ply

3 — Southdown — handcarded/ worsted-spun from the card/ 2-ply

2 — Southdown — handcarded/ woolen-spun from rolags/ 2-ply

DORSET HORN AND POLL DORSET

Dorset Horn and Poll Dorset sheep are almost identical except for the horns part. All Dorset Horn sheep, both male and female, have horns, which curl or curve forward toward their faces; Poll Dorset sheep have no horns. The wool of these two breeds is pretty much indistinguishable. Some say Poll Dorsets aren't as hardy or intelligent as Dorset Horns. In the background of both breeds is a cross between Spanish sheep and native English stock from the 1500s. In Australia, the Poll Dorset was developed by crossing Corriedale and Ryeland sheep and then crossing the lambs from this cross with a Dorset Horn sheep. The resulting Poll lambs were then crossed with Dorset Horn ewes. Those Poll lambs were crossed again with the Purebred Dorset Horn ewes so that a sheep with near 100% Dorset blood was accomplished with all of the Dorset Horn characteristics except for the horns. Meanwhile, in the United States at around the same time, the Poll version of this Dorset breed was being developed just by selecting for a horn-free mutation in a flock in North Carolina.

Dorset Horns were one of the very earliest sheep to have a breed registry; begun in 1892, the society was surely helped to grow by its first patroness, Queen Victoria. In 1890, Dorset Horns were imported to the United States' West Coast. In the 1950s, the Poll Dorset emerged in Australia. The Poll Dorset now well outnumbers its Dorset Horn cousins in England, Australia, and the United States, and Dorset Horns are actually now on the endangered sheep lists in both Britain and the United States.

These sheep are very easy to raise in a wide variety of climates and elevations. They can be bred year-round and may have three births in a two-year time span, making them attractive to shepherds interested in meat production. (Most other sheep breeds have the ability to lamb only once a year, in the spring.)

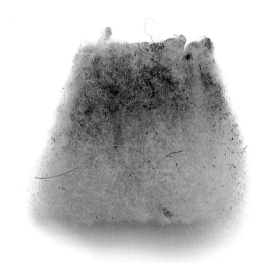

1

— *Dorset Horn* —
handcarded
worsted-spun with
short forward draw
from cigars/
2-ply

Sampling Dorset Horns and Poll Dorsets

For these samples, I used wool from the horned version of Dorset, though this breed is on The Livestock Conservancy list as of 2013, and so the Poll Dorset may be more easily acquired for spinning. I used handcards for all of the samples shown here, but treated the carded wool differently in each case.

❶ & ❷ 2-ply spun with a short forward draw. By spinning these two samples with a short forward draw, I created a yarn that is somewhat worsted. I spun the one below right off the card, so the fibers are all aligned. This yarn is smooth and only slightly elastic. Because the yarn has a hard feeling, the knitted swatch I made with it is a fabric that would be great for outerwear or other hard-wearing items. I spent a little time rubbing the fabric, and no pills formed from the abrasion. This is a great fabric, but I wouldn't want it next to my skin. I spun the other worsted-spun sample opposite from fiber cigars (see page 159), so in this yarn, too, the fibers are mostly aligned. The yarn feels very similar to the first. I wove a swatch with this yarn and can imagine a skirt or jacket made with this fabric.

Spinning these two 2-ply yarns with less twist in the singles would surely have made them softer, but because this would also have made them less hardy, they would have pilled more easily. My goal for worsted-spun Down yarns is strength and durability, which is reduced when you give the yarns less twist.

2

— *Dorset Horn* —
handcarded/
worsted-spun with
short forward draw
from the card/
2-ply

❸ 2-ply spun with a supported long draw. This yarn is the most traditional: I handcarded the wool, then removed the batt from the carder as a rolag, which I spun from the end. This sample is the complete opposite of the worsted-spun samples. It is soft and has drape, though some body remains in the sample. The thick-and-thin spots in the singles are mostly hidden in the swatch knit with the 2-ply yarn, but I think a 3-ply would have been even better. The knitted swatch is very resilient, and would make a great fabric for a cardigan. Within a short time of rubbing, my abrasion test showed some fibers pulling out, which will form pills. Though this yarn has a similar amount of twist as the worsted-drafted samples, the difference in durability is very obvious.

❹ Yarn spun from handmade roving. This yarn is sort of a middle ground between the true woolen sample that was spun with a woolen draft from a rolag and the samples that were spun as worsted from carded fibers. This sample stands up a bit better to the abrasion test, and the yarn is airy and lofty. Though I love the swatch spun from rolags with a supported long draw, this sample might be a good compromise. I stacked carded fibers, pulled them into a roving, and then spun them using a supported long draw. The yarn, even spun with the same whorl and twist, is not as soft as the version spun from rolags, possibly because the latter's fibers spiral into the forming yarn, thus trapping more air than happens with the drawn-out, somewhat-aligned fibers of a roving.

3

— *Dorset Horn* —
*handcarded/
woolen-spun from
rolags
with supported
long draw/
2-ply*

4

— *Dorset Horn* —
*handcarded/
woolen-spun from
roving made from
stacked batts using
supported long draw/
2-ply*

BLACK WELSH MOUNTAIN

Black Welsh Mountain is a dual-purpose breed with a true black fleece, which can be very difficult to find. Although the tips may get a bit bleached by the sun and turn to a slightly reddish color, the fleece is truly black, not dark brown. Breeds with only white wool are generally the most sought after in the wool industry, because white wool, which can be dyed any color, is more versatile in the garment and other industries that use wool. Black, on the other hand, is always black. Because of this, black lambs of many breeds are usually culled, so their black-wool genetics don't contaminate future generations, and so their wool does not contaminate the entire clip during shearing. But Black Welsh Mountains are prized for their black fleece. The wool is great for blending with other natural colors to obtain shading, and as it is a true black, it doesn't need to be dyed when you want black cloth.

The direct ancestors of Black Welsh Mountain sheep are the Welsh Mountain, or White Welsh Mountain, breed. Black Welsh Mountains were developed from this breed by selecting for color over time, until these black sheep were eventually recognized as their own breed. Although the breed description doesn't specify height, most of them are small, about 30 inches tall at the shoulder.

The texture of the adult sheep's wool is medium to coarse, but lamb fleeces can be quite soft, suitable for next-to-skin wear. Staple length is generally 2 to 4 inches, with fleeces weighing between 2½ and 5½ pounds. The fiber diameter ranges between 28 and 36 microns. The range is very similar to that of the Suffolks, though I found the carded Black Welsh to be crisper feeling than Suffolk wool.

As is typical of Down-type wools, the crimp is generally difficult to see in the locks, but the fleece has bounce and extreme loft, though my samples didn't have as much elasticity as I found in other Down-type breeds. The wool is dense, with blocky locks that are hard to distinguish from one another, but it almost always has less kemp than what you find in its ancestors, the White Welsh Mountain. Because the fleece is fairly low in grease content, it's very easy to scour. The staple length is on the shorter side, but if you find a fleece with longer locks, you can comb it, if you wish. It can be used for household goods, including carpets, but it is soft enough for clothing as well. In spite of its crispness in comparison with some others in this category, I found myself spinning a wide variety of samples with it.

Sampling Black Welsh Mountain

❶ & ❷ 3-ply spun from rolags. These are the samples that I would consider the most conventionally spun, or, in other words, spun taking the approach I would consider most likely to work best with this wool. Both of these 3-ply yarns were carded, made into rolags, and then spun using a supported long draw. The only difference between them is the thickness of the singles. Sample 1, knit with the finer singles, is a denser fabric. The yarn, though not harsh feeling, also feels denser. A rub test on the corner of the swatch indicates that this fabric will last a long time. Although it's not a fabric I'd choose for a cuddly sweater, I could see it used for great boot socks or a nice, lighter-weight work sweater. Sample 2, made with the thicker singles, is much bouncier, and the knit swatch also has a lot more bounce than the other. I can see a basic pullover out of this yarn to be worn over another shirt for winter wear. This fabric did show a bit of wear when I rubbed the corner of it, but its warmth is unmistakable.

When I was spinning these yarns, I was not in love with the fiber, perhaps because I spun it immediately after working with one of the finer wools. When I knit the yarns into swatches, however, the yarns were transformed, and I could see why this wool was developed.

1 *Black Welsh — Mountain — handcarded/worsted-spun from rolags using supported long draw/3-ply*

2 *Black Welsh — Mountain — handcarded/woolen-spun from rolags using supported long draw/3-ply*

❸ 2-ply spun from stacked handcarded batts. For these yarns, I handcarded the wool, which I removed from the cards without rolling and then stacked, so that I could pull the fleece out from the side to make roving (for more about this carding method, see page 161). I rarely stack more than five or six batts when I use this technique.

When the batts were the thickness I wanted, I spun them in a worsted manner and made a 2-ply yarn with the singles. I find it a bit more difficult to get a consistent yarn using this method than when spinning supported long draw from rolags, but both the yarn and knitted fabric are somewhat softer. This yarn, as well as the two yarns just discussed, would make a good woven fabric for a warm winter coat.

3 *Black Welsh — Mountain — handcarded/worsted-spun from roving made from stacked batts using supported long draw/2-ply*

❹ 2-ply spun from fiber cigars. For this sample, I handcarded the fleece and then formed each batt into a fiber cigar by rolling it opposite to the way I'd make a rolag (see page 159). This approach keeps the fibers pretty well lined up. I spun the cigars with a short forward draw. The kemp in my sample was trapped and compacted with the rest of the fibers, resulting in a yarn that turned out to be a bit harsh; in fact, the swatch I wove with it feels like burlap.

(I didn't make a knitted swatch.) Although it's not a yarn I'd want to use for clothing, it could make a great shopping bag or carpeting.

4 Black Welsh
— Mountain —
handcarded/worsted-
spun from cigars
using short forward
draw/2-ply

❺ 2-ply spun from the end of a card. For sample 5, I again handcarded the wool, but this time I spun the fibers right off the end of the card and then made a 2-ply yarn. Lots of the kemp stayed in the pins of the card, and even more came off as I spun. Since I used a drafting method very close to short forward draw, I expected a yarn more similar to the one I spun from fiber cigars. Instead, the yarn is a bit softer and would be just fine for use in both woven and knit garments. Although, as I've said before, Down-type fibers wouldn't be my first choice for a lace project, I'm very happy with the lace swatch opposite. The holes of the lace remain open, making the lace pattern easy to see. The fabric has plenty of body, and though

it wouldn't drape in the same way some lace patterns require, the yarn would make a great sweater with a lace design worked into it.

❻ Combed Black Welsh Mountain yarn. I couldn't resist trying combs on this fiber and sharing the results, even though combs aren't the focus of this section. I spun the fiber right off the comb using a worsted draw, which removed almost all the kemp and made it much easier to spin a fine yarn. I wish you could all feel this sample. (You can, if you make one for yourself!) Both the yarn and the lace fabric I made with it feel almost silky. In the knitted swatch, you can see that the lace pattern is open and quite visible. It's hard to believe that this yarn and swatch are from the same fleece as the swatch I made from the worsted-spun fiber cigar on the previous page. I am so excited about these samples that I have big plans to hunt down a fleece so that I can spin some yarn like this to make a sweater for myself.

The wide range of fiber diameters available from this breed means that it's possible to find a natural black fleece for any project you might want. And as you can see from my experiments (which were not at all exhaustive), you should be easily able to find a prep and spinning method to suit the outcome you desire.

5 Black Welsh
— Mountain —
handcarded/worsted-
spun off the card
using short forward
draw/2-ply

6 Black Welsh
— Mountain —
combed/
worsted-spun from
the comb/
2-ply

Chapter 7

MULTI-COATED

BREEDS

A MULTICOATED SHEEP is one with both an outercoat and an undercoat. Some even have in-between fibers that are easy to manage, but they could also be kemp, which can be challenging. A wiry fiber, kemp looks very much like crimpy hair, is usually quite thick, and doesn't show dyed colors well. Although some of it tends to fall out while you're spinning, not all of it does.

The locks of fleeces in this category are generally triangular, wider at the cut end and coming to a point just where the tips of the outercoat come together. Because of this shape, the coats can be easily separated by hand. It's difficult to make generalizations about crimp, because each breed has its own characteristic crimp structure. The strong outercoats of Karakul and Scottish Blackface have no obvious crimp, for example, whereas the crimp of their undercoats isn't uniform over the length of the fiber.

One of the great things about multicoated breeds is that the fleece from a single sheep offers a range of possibilities to work with. The outer coat of Scottish Blackface, for instance, is very strong, with a micron count of up to 40 microns and sometimes even more. You can use these fibers for items like rope, dog leashes, and horse tack. On the other hand, the fibers of Scottish Blackface's undercoat can be very fine, appropriate for knitted and woven garments. In addition, not all outercoats of multicoated sheep are as coarse as those of Scottish Blackface. Many Shetland and Icelandic fleeces, for example, have an outercoat fine enough for next-to-skin wear.

Characteristics of MULTICOATED BREEDS

Icelandic

Origin: Brought to Iceland by the Vikings between 870 and 930 CE

Fleece weight: 4–7 lbs.

Staple length: 4"–18"

Fiber diameter: 19–31 microns, over both coats

Lock characteristics: Long, triangular

Color: Wide range

Karakul

Origin: Deserts of Central Asia

Fleece weight: 5–10 lbs.

Staple length: 6"–12"

Fiber diameter: 25–36 microns

Lock characteristics: Triangular

Color: Grays, browns, blacks, some white

Navajo Churro

Origin: Spanish Churra brought by explorers to North America in the 15th and 16th centuries

Fleece weight: 4–8 lbs.

Staple length: 4"–12"

Fiber diameter: 10–35 microns, with kemp at about 65 microns

Lock characteristics: Triangular, distinct locks

Color: Wide range

Sara Lamb spun and wove this fabric with Shetland fiber.

Scottish Blackface

Origin: **Scotland**
Fleece weight: **3–6½ lbs.**
Staple length: **6"–14"**
Fiber diameter: **28–40 microns**
Lock characteristics: **Long, triangular, with kemp**
Color: **White**

Shetland

Origin: **Shetland Islands**
Fleece weight: **2–5 lbs.**
Staple length: **2"–10"**
Fiber diameter: **20–30 microns**
Lock characteristics: **Dense, triangular**
Color: **One of the widest ranges of any breed**

Romanov

Origin: **Near Moscow**
Fleece weight: **6–13 lbs.**
Staple length: **4"–5"**
Fiber diameter: **16–150 microns**
Lock characteristics: **Short, blocky, triangular**
Color: **Gray**

Working with the Multicoats

You can separate the coats before or after scouring — or not at all. The fibers do slide away from each other a bit more easily, however, if they are clean. Deciding whether or not to separate the coats at all depends on what kind of yarn you want. For harder-wearing yarns, as well as less prep work, not separating them is the way to go. Traditional lopi yarn, for example, consists of both coats of Icelandic wool loosely spun together, making a beautiful, hard-wearing yarn. Blending the outer- and undercoats also makes for a more resilient yarn, since when bent, the generally stronger outercoat fibers seem to work harder to get back to their original configuration than the softer, finer undercoat fibers, and that energy contributes bounce to the yarn.

The fun part of spinning these dual-coated breeds is that you get to make so many choices. The drawback, however, is that you can be paralyzed by the choices and unable to know where to begin. The answer to this dilemma (as usual) is to sample. Always make sure to get a few extra ounces of fleece to allow for sampling so that you can be sure that the project you have envisioned is going to work out the way you imagine it. In addition, take the opportunity to learn how each coat behaves on its own, as well as together, in a finished fabric. If you don't have a project in mind when you begin spinning, these swatches will speak to you and tell you what the most beautiful end result will be.

Spinning the Undercoat Alone

The undercoat of many dual-coated breeds is extremely soft and downy, and lends itself to many next-to-skin items, as well as lace and undergarments. The crimp of the undercoat of these breeds is generally not organized in the lock, though it is quite obvious when you look at the fibers individually. This unorganized crimp pushes each fiber away from its neighbors, suggesting a woolen-style spinning that makes the most of the bounce built into the fibers. On the other hand, you can choose to use a worsted draft, in order to add hardiness to the yarn and help it resist the felting that occurs because of the short fibers.

Spinning the Outer Coat Alone

The crimp of the outercoat of multicoat breeds is generally almost nonexistent. If you spin the outercoat by itself, you'll get a dense, very hard-wearing yarn. This lends itself well to a worsted-style spinning, which takes advantage of and builds on the strength already there in the fibers.

Spinning the Two Coats Together

If you decide to spin the under- and outercoats together, the preferred method is woolen for both prepping and spinning. For prepping, because of the differing lengths of the coats, handcombs and flick carders cause more waste than is necessary, whereas handcards work the coats evenly, making a beautifully blended batt or rolag. The reason for spinning woolen rather than worsted-style is that the short drafts and smoothing motions you use when you spin worsted tend to draw out all the longer fibers and leave the softer undercoat behind, which you don't want to do. A woolen draft, on the other hand, allows all of the fibers to be taken up by the twist and enter the yarn together evenly.

If you prefer to comb the fleece of the dual-coated breeds, using a single-pitch set is key to keeping the different lengths together. Follow the combing method described for multipitched combs (see page 115), but use as few passes as possible.

Working with More than Two Coats

You can't always separate all three coats when the fleece you have has more than two types of fiber. Often, the third type of fiber is kemp — generally short, wirelike fibers with little bends in them. They do fall out during processing and spinning, but you generally don't lose all of them. Because kemp adds a bit of a prickle factor, fleeces with a lot of kemp are not recommended to be worn near the neck or other sensitive areas. Don't discount the use of the wool, however, just because a bit of kemp is present in a fleece.

SEPARATING THE COATS

Here are a few options for how to separate the double coats.

Do it by hand. Gently hold the cut end of the lock and pull the tips of the longer fibers (a). I like to line up the pile of outercoat fibers as I separate them, so that they're ready and easy to spin without any additional preparation. You can card the short, fine fibers left in your hand or just spin them from the cloud after the longer fibers are all removed to your satisfaction.

The cloud refers to fibers that are not all aligned and have had less prep than either roving or top. The locks have been opened either by hand or machine, and the wool is then simply spun by the handful, with no regard for where the fibers are coming from within the mass (b).

By hand (a)

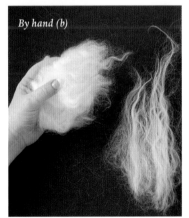

By hand (b)

Use a comb as an anchor. Load the locks onto one 2-pitch comb, letting the comb be an anchor that holds onto the butts while you remove the longer fibers with your other hand.

Using a comb

Comb with another comb. Load the locks onto one 2-pitch comb, then use the other comb to pull the fibers out. The short fibers will stay in the first comb, as the longer fibers move to the working comb.

AMERICAN KARAKUL

Karakul sheep are one of the oldest domesticated sheep breeds in the world, part of a breed group called fat-tailed sheep. Mosaics from 3000 BCE include pictures of fat-tailed sheep. Generally found in Asia, northern Africa, and the Middle East, they make up about 25 percent of the world's sheep population. Karakul is the only true fat-tailed sheep in the United States, and although American Karakul bears a resemblance to its Middle Eastern cousins, some differences are due to its importation to the United States.

Karakul has been raised for hundreds of years, mainly for fur. Fetal and newborn lambs have a curled wool coat that lies tight and flat to the skin. In the Middle East, these lamb skins have always been used for garments. In the early 1900s, a few shepherds decided to import some Karakul sheep in order to produce these furs in the United States. C. C. Young in Texas imported sheep three times between 1908 and 1914. Importations continued through about 1929 in both the United States and Canada, but Karakul numbers were too few to achieve the goals of serious Persian lamb production, even when imported Karakuls were crossed with some available sheep to produce pelts. The positive outcome is the development of the American Karakul as a distinct breed. Although the breed is quite variable, due to geography and the many different crosses in flocks across North America, many of the characteristic Karakul traits were retained.

Handspinners can find a wide range of colors, textures, and coats, including both single and dual coats. If you're a spinner who likes naturally dark colors, Karakul is a great resource. The dual-coated fleeces are a bit more difficult to separate than those of some other multicoat breeds, because Karakul's finer coat can sometimes be about the same length as the coarser outercoat. Its undercoat always surprises me, however, as it feels quite soft, often comparable to some Corriedale.

If you do spin the coats together, this is not a wool to wear against sensitive skin, but you can use it for a wide range of other things. It's

great for felted projects; felt from this wool is very strong and long lasting. Socks made from it seem to refuse to wear out; in fact, it's the typical wool used for socks in the Middle East.

As with most of the fleeces I describe here, the individuals within a given breed can show a lot of variety, and therefore, if you're looking for a fleece with a soft undercoat, it's best to find one that you can examine in person, or find a supplier you trust to help you choose the fleece for your project.

One processed Karakul that's available on the market is lovely to spin and has a wonderful feel. The coats are processed together, however, so if you are looking for just the soft undercoat, purchasing a raw fleece is currently the only way to get it. If you wish, you can purchase a fleece and send it to a mill that has de-hairing equipment. You'll get back both coats, machine separated and ready for your project.

Sampling American Karakul

The sample yarns I show here demonstrate both separated coats and coats carded together.

❶ **Unseparated coats.** This extremely strong yarn also has plenty of bounce and elasticity. I did not separate the coats, but instead carded rolags, then spun using a woolen draft and made a 3-ply yarn. The yarn isn't as coarse as might be expected, but it does have bit of a halo, due to the fibers in the coarser outercoat that don't like to bend easily. This feature is what gives the yarn its great loft. Though I sampled it only in a knit swatch, I can also see it used in a woven project if you need durability.

❷ **Outercoat only.** For this yarn, I separated the coats by hand and spun the outercoat without combing, flicking, or carding the fibers: I just picked them up and spun them with a woolen draft and made a 2-ply yarn. I kept the twist down a bit, but knowing that I was making an extremely coarse yarn intended for weaving, I added a bit more twist than I would have for a yarn spun with this fiber that I planned to knit with. The woven swatch is quite strong, not good for clothing but great for strong bags, straps, and leashes. Such a fabric would last for years and years.

❸ **Undercoat only.** Here's a yarn that is likely to be a surprise to everyone new to this breed. After I separated the fibers, I combed the undercoat and spun it from the comb with a worsted, short forward draw and then made a 2-ply yarn. Maybe the yarn isn't as soft as Cormo, but it is unexpectedly soft, and most people would be fine with a cardigan made from this yarn. It would also be great as a heavy lace yarn.

Why Fat-Tailed?

Fat-tailed sheep are so called because of the fat stores that they carry along their backs and on either side of their tails, needed because they usually live in more arid places, and extra moisture is stored in the fat. Think camel, but with the storage at the back end. American Tunis developed from crosses of fat-tailed breeds with European breeds and therefore has some fat-tailed qualities.

1 — Karakul —
unseparated/
handcarded/
woolen-spun from
rolags/
3-ply

2 — Karakul —
outercoat separated
by hand (no further
prep)/woolen-spun
from the cloud/
2-ply

3 — Karakul —
combed undercoat/
worsted-spun
from the comb
using short
forward draw/
2-ply

SCOTTISH BLACKFACE

Records of these sheep date back to 1504, when James IV of Scotland established a flock of five thousand Scottish Blackface sheep in the Borders (a region that included southern Scotland and part of what is now England). In 1861, the first Scottish Blackface were imported into the United States, specifically into New York Mills, New York; other flocks spread from there. Although these sheep are found all over Scotland, the Scottish islands, and Northern Ireland (their wool still accounts for 40 percent of the wool production in Scotland and between 20 and 30 percent in all of Great Britain), they remain a minor breed in the United States. It is a small-bodied sheep prized for its meat and resistance to disease. Depending on where you are, you'll discover that this breed has many different names,

including Linton, Scottish Mountain, Scottish Highland, Scotch Blackface, Scotch Horn, and, in Kerry, Ireland, Blackfaced Highland. Any sheep with that many names must be very important.

Another multicoated breed with an extremely coarse outercoat, Scottish Blackface has a somewhat fine to medium undercoat and an abundance of kemp. I've spun this wool quite a bit and haven't found a way to separate the coats well enough to remove all the kemp, though combing does remove quite a bit of it. These fleeces are generally not the ones that handspinners gravitate to for their day-to-day spinning or for next-to-skin wear projects, but the wool does have some benefits. The yarn is appropriate for both woven and knitted fabrics that are hard wearing. The outercoat of this fleece is extremely strong, and therefore may be just what you are looking for if you're making a dog leash or collar, a nice belt, or those ropes you need for your farm gates.

The fibers are extraordinarily springy, making them desirable for high-quality wool carpets, most notably Wilton carpets. This wool recovers even after being pressed down for extended periods of time by heavy furniture. Find me a synthetic fiber that can do that! This tendency to spring back makes the wool great for stuffing mattresses and pillows. The softer fleeces are also used to make the famous Harris Tweed, a handwoven fabric from the Outer Hebrides.

Sampling Scottish Blackface

❶ 2-ply blended coats. I made this first sample by blending both coats together on combs and then spinning the yarn right from the comb with a worsted draw. As I combed and spun this fiber, lots of kemp fell out, although some did remain in the yarn. In spite of that, this is the softest yarn and swatch of the three I made with this fleece, and I believe that softness is the result of this preparation method. The swatch also has a very nice luster, and the fabric would make a fine cardigan, though it probably isn't next-to-skin soft enough for most people.

❷ 2-ply laceweight outercoat. I separated the coats of the fleece for this yarn by hand, then combed the outercoat fibers and pulled them from the comb without a diz. I used a woolen draft when I spun the resulting combed top. Though I've written a lot about how great the coarser outercoats can be for straps, leashes, and ropes, I wanted to see what would happen if I made lace from this yarn, and as it turns out, the lace is beautiful. It has some halo and shows very little kemp. It doesn't hold the blocking as long as I would like, but I think it would make a great table runner or fireplace mantel scarf.

❸ 3-ply bulky undercoat. For this sample, I worked with the undercoat fibers that I separated from the outercoat used for the laceweight yarn (2). I handcarded the wool, then spun from rolags using a supported long draw. The handcarding kept all of the kemp in place, evenly blending the soft fibers with this tough kemp to make the prickliest and scratchiest of all of the samples. If I had to choose one thing I would use this yarn for, it would be a rug and nothing else.

1
Scottish
— Blackface —
combed blended
coats/worsted-
spun from the
comb/2-ply

2
Scottish
— Blackface —
separated by hand/
combed outercoat/
handmade top/no
diz/worsted-spun/
2-ply/laceweight

3
Scottish
— Blackface —
separated by hand/
handcarded undercoat/
spun from rolags
using supported long
draw/3-ply

SHETLAND

Shetland is considered a primitive, or unimproved, breed, which means that it has not been crossed with other breeds in order to develop a particular trait, such as increased body size, better wool production, or superior fertility. Though I've categorized it here as a multicoated breed, some Shetlands are single coated, some double coated, and others somewhere in between. One of the most wonderful things about this breed is the variability from sheep to sheep, even on the same farm.

In their book *In Sheep's Clothing: A Handspinner's Guide to Wool*, Nola and Jane Fournier classify Shetland fleece as a Down-type fiber because of its similarity in both crimp and feel to some of the other Down-type wools. Shetlands are so varied, however, that it's hard to pin them down to just one type. Because different shepherds have different goals for their flocks, the traits they choose to develop vary as well. This is why you'll find spinners who think Shetland is the softest wool to be found and other spinners who say they've tried it and found it so very scratchy. You'll need to evaluate individual fleeces and make your own decision about each, based on its particular qualities.

Shetland locks are pointed and triangular shaped, with very good crimp. The yarn is bouncy and lofty. Fiber diameters vary even over the bodies of individual Shetlands (as well as of many other primitive sheep). Fiber at the neck and shoulder is the finest at 10 to 20 microns, and as we move toward the back of the sheep, it continues to get a bit stronger, until finally at the back end it's 25 to 35 microns As you can see, if you separate a Shetland fleece according to its location on the body, you may have a wide range of fibers to work with, including those for the softest shawls to those best used for hard-wearing outerwear and rugs. Fleece that's on the very fine end of the spectrum is spun to knit the Shetland shawls known as wedding-ring shawls, which are so very fine that they can be drawn through a ring.

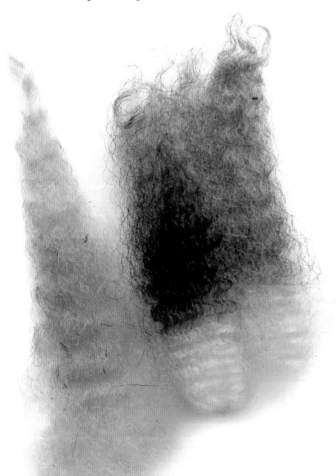

Not only are there single-coated and multi-coated Shetlands with different fleece qualities, but these sheep also come in many different colors: 11 main colors with shades in between and 33 different recognized markings. This is what has the made the wool perfect for all those beautiful, natural-colored Fair Isle sweaters.

Sampling Shetland

I was dancing happy with all of the yarns that came from this fleece, which was a true double coat.

❶ 2-ply blended coats. The undercoat of this fleece was only about 2 inches shorter than the outercoat, so I combed the sample, not worrying that the coats would separate and the undercoat would be left behind as waste. (I was concerned about this when I worked with the Icelandic fleece, in which there's a much larger difference in the fiber lengths; see pages 210–211.) After combing, I dizzed the top straight from the combs and spun worsted-style. The blended yarn is very soft, resilient, and wonderful to touch. Although the yarn doesn't have a lot of elasticity, the knitted swatch is very elastic. This is a fine yarn that could be used for lace, a very fine-gauge knitted fabric, or a wonderful woven garment. Most commercially processed Shetland contains blended coats and gives a lovely yarn similar to what I have produced here from the raw fleece.

❷ 2-ply outercoat. This Shetland's outercoat is definitely stronger than its undercoat, but not what I would call scratchy. I separated the outercoat by hand, then spun with no further preparation, using a worsted-style draft and keeping the twist low in both the singles and the ply. The sett on this woven sample, like that for all of the others in the book, was 10 ends per inch (epi), which I found to be too wide a sett for this particular yarn. I also wove the sample extremely loosely, and then finished it aggressively in hot water. This finishing brought up the halo, softened the hand of the woven fabric, and brought the yarns a bit closer. Even though I think a sett of 12 to 15 epi would have made this fabric a bit nicer, I was a convert after finishing it in hot water.

❸ 2-ply undercoat. After separating the undercoat, I again began spinning with no further prep, but this time, I used a woolen technique. I was not prepared to like this yarn as much as I do. It is not the most consistent yarn, which is what I prefer for lace, but the hand of both the yarn and the fabric is just wonderful. Sadly, that is very difficult to convey in words and photos, so I encourage you to make these samples for yourself, changing the amount of twist to see how that affects your results. The yarn and swatch I made here would not qualify for wedding-ring-shawl status, but the yarn is desirable nonetheless.

Due to its variability, including its range of textures, fleece types, and colors, Shetland is a wool that could spur a study all its own. Just collecting and sampling fleeces from all over the world could take years before you'd see what this breed really can do.

3 — *Shetland* —
undercoat hand separated/ woolen-spun no further prep/ 2-ply

2 — *Shetland* —
outercoat hand separated/ worsted (low twist) spun with no further prep/ 2-ply

1 — *Shetland* —
combed blended coats and dizzed/ worsted-spun/ 2-ply

ICELANDIC

We've learned about dual-purpose sheep. Well, Icelandic sheep are triple purpose! Milk, wool, and meat: What more could we want? Modern Icelandic sheep are direct descendants of the sheep brought to Iceland by Viking settlers in the ninth and tenth centuries. Without these sheep, the Icelandic human population would not have survived. The sheep thrive with grazing in the summer and hay in the winter; no grain is required to raise these hardy sheep.

Most shepherds of Icelandic sheep shear twice a year. In most primitive sheep, a natural break in the fiber occurs because of natural shedding, and it's best to shear before the break happens. Shedded fleece has to be collected in clumps, whereas shearing is faster, and it keeps the fleece intact and thus more desirable.

Icelandic sheep are dual coated as well as triple purpose. Their medium outercoat

is called *tog,* meaning "coarse wool," and the very soft undercoat is called *thel,* which means "fine wool." The two coats together provide a very warm fleece for the sheep of cold, windy Iceland. The yarn that's made by loosely spinning the two coats together is known as lopi, a medium wool that's wonderful for sweaters, warm shawls, and other outerwear, as well as for felting. The long outercoat fibers spin nicely into a worsted yarn that is long lasting, slow to pill, and great for a strong weaving warp. You can also use this yarn for ropes, carpets, and other utilitarian objects. The short, fine undercoat fibers have a very inconsistent crimp. Because they are so short, they should be spun with a moderate amount of twist. Yarns spun from the undercoat are wonderful for next-to-skin use and fine lace projects.

Sampling Icelandic

The samples here are exactly what you would expect from Icelandic wool.

❶ 3-ply blended coats. I handcarded both coats together, made them into rolags, and then spun the rolags using a woolen method and plied it into a 3-ply yarn. This yarn is perfect for a wide range of things. The singles could be spun a bit finer for delicate knitted or woven fabrics. Though the coarser outercoat fibers are included, this fabric would be very comfortable against my neck, and because of the strength of the fibers, the blend would make very durable socks. I can see from this sample why the people in Iceland get by with only one breed of sheep. I could be very happy with this wool!

1 — Icelandic —
blended coats
handcarded/
woolen-spun from
rolags/
3-ply

2 — Icelandic —
outercoat hand
separated and combed/
worsted-spun
(medium twist)/2-ply

❷ 2-ply outercoat. I separated the under- and outercoats by hand (no tools), but then combed the outercoat fibers to improve their alignment. I then spun with a worsted draft and a medium twist. The angle of the twist in the ply is about 35 degrees. This yarn would be perfect for carpet warp. It is inelastic, hard to break with my hands, and will be extremely hard wearing. You could spin it with even less twist, but because it's so strong, I'm not sure what the purpose would be: I wouldn't consider this fiber spun on its own to be something I'd make garments out of. Notice the color difference in the outercoat compared to the undercoat. This yarn is a lot less gray than the other yarns. The gray in the blended swatch comes mostly from the undercoat, though you can see some gray fibers peeking through in the woven swatch.

❸ 2-ply undercoat. This wool is light as a feather. I spun the fibers worsted right after removing the outercoat. No teasing, combing, or any other prep method was necessary. This 2-ply yarn has a medium twist. Though the yarn doesn't have a lot of elasticity, it is very resilient and airy. The lace swatch is just perfect in its drape. I could see spinning this into a 3-ply yarn for a very fine-gauge sweater or for baby things.

Icelandic wool seems to be a perfect combination of strength and softness that will take you anywhere you'd like to go in your spinning and fabric making.

3

*Icelandic —
undercoat hand
separated/worsted-
spun from the cloud
(medium twist)/
2-ply*

Chapter 8

OTHER

BREEDS

I'VE RESERVED THIS CHAPTER FOR WOOLS that don't easily fit anywhere else. Some are primitive breeds that slough off (shed) their wool each year and some are newer breeds that have been developed by crossing one or more breeds coming from different categories. The result is that they have characteristics from more than one group and don't fit well into any one.

This also means, however, that we have a huge opportunity to experiment with how we prepare the fibers of these breeds. With other breeds, we focused on one preparation method, while changing the drafting method to get different yarns. I chose each prep because I felt it was the best way to get the most beneficial outcome from that fiber. This is not the only approach to prepping and spinning, however, and in this chapter you'll see that you can process wools using a variety of different tools, or no tools at all. In some areas of the world where spinning happens every day, for example, there are no fiber prep tools, and fingers and hands are what are used. The resulting yarns are beautiful and useful.

The three breeds I sample in this chapter are very different from each other. If you look closely, however, you can see ways that they are similar to breeds discussed earlier in the book. When you choose the way to prepare their fiber, you can take advantage of this information when you detect similarities to those earlier fibers and proceed accordingly.

Characteristics of the "OTHER" BREEDS

California Red

Origin: American Tunis/Barbados Blackbelly
Fleece weight: 5-7 lbs.
Staple length: 3"-6"
Fiber diameter: 28-31 microns
Lock characteristics: Blocky, with disorganized crimp
Color: Whites

Jacob

Origin: Unknown
Fleece weight: 3-6 lbs
Staple length: 3"-7"
Fiber diameter: 25-35 microns
Lock characteristics: Pointed, dense, may be some kemp
Color: White/black, brown/white, lilac/white

Soay

Origin: Islands of Soay and Hirta (off Scotland)
Fleece weight: ¾-2 lbs.
Staple length: 1.4"-4"
Fiber diameter: 9-48 microns
Lock characteristics: Blocky, sometimes double coated, variable
Color: Browns

Gulf Coast

Origin: Brought to southeastern United States by early explorers
Fleece weight: 4-6 lbs.
Staple length: 2½"-4"
Fiber diameter: 26-32 microns
Lock characteristics: Blocky, uneven crimp
Color: Mostly white, some tan, brown, black

Santa Cruz

Origin: Feral from Santa Cruz island off California coast
Fleece weight: Less than 2 lbs.
Staple length: 2"-4"
Fiber diameter: 18-26 microns
Lock characteristics: Blocky, short, bouncy, dense
Color: Whites, browns

Tunis

Origin: Tunisian Barbary/Southdown and possibly English Leicester
Fleece weight: 6-15 lbs.
Staple length: 4"-6"
Fiber diameter: 24-31 microns
Lock characteristics: Open and distinct, pointed tips
Color: Creamy ivory

Using Dog-Grooming Tools

If you don't have access to tools made specifically for wool preparation, you can use dog-grooming tools in a pinch. They'll work, though not as well as the tools made especially for the job. You can use a pet comb in place of a flicker if you plan on dragging the tool through the fibers to open them up. You can also use two pet slickers in place of handcards while you figure out which handcards to buy. The teeth on the dog slickers are not as strong as those on wool carding cloth, so they will break down more quickly. While it's true that these slickers are about 10 percent of the cost of a good pair of handcards, a good set of handcards will last a lifetime if you give them proper care.

Hand Prepping Your Fleece

Fingers and hands are marvelous things. We type with them and hold things with them and tickle with them. They are great tools, too, but I think we sometimes forget this. For some of the samples in this portion of the book, all that I used to prep the fiber for spinning after washing were my fingers. I simply picked the wool open with my fingers and spun from the "cloud" of fibers that formed. The cloud that is formed by pulling the locks completely apart gives a beautiful and very woolen-style yarn, but it's difficult to get a very consistent yarn this way. Opening the locks just a bit at the cut end and spinning from there will give a more consistent thread. Whichever you decide, this preparation method works best with shorter-stapled fibers. It isn't the best method for staple lengths of more than 6 inches, but I encourage you to experiment and see what you think. As with the other preparation methods, your approach depends on what kind of yarn you want to spin and what purpose it will serve. Sampling and swatching are your friends in every case. There are two ways to hand prep your fleece.

Separating tips and cut ends by hand (a). Take about a handful of fiber and start pulling lightly to open the fiber tips and cut ends. Separate the fibers from each other so there is space and air in between. Make sure to pull the fibers apart from each other so that there won't be any lumps when you begin to spin. The yarn you get from this prep will be very much like a yarn prepared with handcards and spun from a rolag, because the fibers will be facing every which way. It may look a little more rustic than the woolen-spun yarn, though, unless you spin it very fine with a tight twist. (See the samples of Jacob yarn on page 223.)

Separating only the cut ends by hand (b). This method takes less time and results in a more consistent yarn. Take a lock and open only the cut end by running it between your thumb and fingertip. This separates any ends that are sticking together due to shearing. When you spin these locks, spin them from the cut end. I used this method with the California Red samples on page 219.

With the second method you can also open the tips of the locks if you wish. Sometimes the tips can seem a bit glued together and a little opening will help to make the yarn even more consistent. Try it both ways and see if opening the tips is necessary.

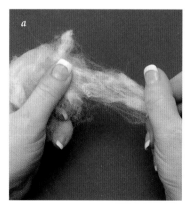
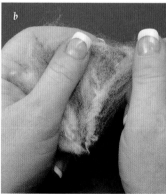

Separating tips and cut ends   *Separating cut ends only*

CALIFORNIA RED

California Red is a very new breed. Glen Spurlock, a shepherd in Davis, California, wanted to produce a wool-free sheep with good body size for meat production. He began by crossing Barbados Blackbelly sheep, a hair breed from the island of Barbados, with Tunis, which has lovely wool. Tunis wool is reddish in the lambs and then fades to white wool in the mature sheep, although their faces remain reddish. The sheep that resulted does have a nice body size for meat production, and furthermore, it can be bred off season like many of the hair-type sheep. This gives the shepherd the potential for having three lamb crops in two years, rather than just one per year, like most breeds with British backgrounds. So, Mr. Spurlock was successful in two of his goals, but fortunately for us, he didn't succeed with his goal of a wool-free sheep.

California Red lambs are born red, and the wool lightens over the first 12 to 18 months, leaving a red coloration on their heads and legs. Their mature wool can be white to cream to beige or oatmeal in color, many times with gold or red hair fibers throughout the fleece. These give a reddish hue to the wool, although you can find some fleeces with very few colored hairs in them. The fibers feel silky and smooth, but the fiber diameter lends the wool to projects that may need a bit more durability than a finer fleece can provide.

Fleeces usually weigh from 5 to 7 pounds with about a 50 percent yield. Average staple length is between 3 and 6 inches, with a very narrow fiber diameter range of 28 to 31 microns. The locks are square and blocky, with good but disorganized crimp, similar to Down-type locks. Because of its crimp structure, lock shape, and fiber loft, in fact, this fleece could easily fit into the Down category, but I chose to place it here, because of the thicker, colored fibers that are found in many of the fleeces, as well as the somewhat pointed locks that some fleeces can have.

Sampling California Red

This fleece does beautifully with any preparation methods, though I chose to use a hand-prep method for the samples shown opposite. My fleece had an abundance of red hairs in it, giving it a cinnamon color, though the wool itself is more beige. The kempy hairs also give the resulting yarn a harsher feel. Combing the fibers would have removed many of the red hairs, making it much softer than the results I got. Other fleeces are available from these sheep with almost no kempy hairs. Base your choice of a fleece on the use and feel you want from your yarn.

❶ **2-ply woolen-spun bulky.** I spun my first sample from the lock with no processing. Notice that this sample isn't as lumpy as the Jacob sample (on page 223), because I opened it very little with my fingers before spinning. I spun the singles with a woolen draft into a fairly bulky yarn and plied to a 2-ply. The resulting yarn is fuzzy and fluffy. The stitch definition is sort of hidden in this swatch because of the woolen spinning style. This may not be the yarn you'd choose to use if you were making a lot of cables and wanted them to show.

❷ **2-ply worsted-spun.** I spun this yarn from the lock with no processing, but for this sample, I spun with a worsted draft. Changing the drafting method really changed the smoothness of the yarn, as well as the face of the stitches in the knitted swatch. Both yarns

feel equally soft, but the worsted-spun yarn is smoother, and the swatch therefore shows better stitch definition, though not as good, however, as it would have been had I used a worsted prep method, like combing.

❸ **2-ply worsted-spun laceweight.** The finest yarn was also not processed before spinning, and I spun it exactly the same way as sample 2. The only difference is that I spun it a bit finer. This sample is much crisper than the other two, and it is also much smoother, though some inconsistency does sneak in. The lace swatch is great; the fiber pushes out and holds the holes open. Though this fabric isn't as soft as one made with the fine wools, it has a lovely drape and would be a great shawl for everyday wear. I wove the swatch on the right to be very open and then finished it with an aggressive wash in hot water. Before finishing, the woven swatch was crisp and a bit coarse, but after the wash it softened immensely. I could see this as a nice fabric for a wide variety of things, from bags to clothing. It doesn't have much spring or elasticity to it, but any kind of jacket or skirt would be lovely. For bags or other items that might get a lot of hard use, I would probably sett the yarns a bit more closely.

California Red seems to be a wonderful cross-breeding accident. Mr. Spurlock didn't achieve his original goal, but we are all benefiting from the actual results.

1 — California Red —
hand opened/
woolen-spun/
2-ply (bulky)

2 — California Red —
hand opened/
worsted-spun/
2-ply

3 — California Red —
hand opened/
worsted-spun/
2-ply laceweight

JACOB

Jacob sheep are sometimes said to have come from biblical Jacob's flock of spotted sheep that he got from his father-in-law. It is difficult to trace the sheep back that far, for sure, but they are indeed a breed that was brought to England from the Middle East. In the 1800s, they were used as ornamental sheep on English estates because of their interesting color patterns and multiple horns.

Their small body size means they're not a great breed for meat production, and their fleeces, too, are small, in addition to being spotted, both characteristics that make them unacceptable for commercial wool production.

They have survived, however, due to their unusual appearance. They are generally black and white, although the softer gray or brown component of the fleece is called *lilac*. Like some of the other more primitive breeds, such as Navajo Churro and Manx Loaghtan, they can have anywhere from two to six horns, but the absence of a dual coat suggests some improvements or crossing with other breeds over time. In fact, in the not-so-distant past, the British Jacobs were bred for larger body size to increase their meat-producing potential. The U.S. Jacobs have been largely unimproved and therefore maintain the historic Jacob size and shape.

The kemp sometimes found in the fleeces is listed as acceptable but not desirable in the breed standard. Although breed societies differ, one of the standards is 60 percent white with 40 percent colored markings, although some fleeces have much greater percentages of one color over the other. You can separate the colors for beautiful, natural-colored colorwork, or you can prepare and spin the fiber to create a blend of colors, from dark to light, all from one fleece.

Fiber diameters range widely from 25 to 35 microns. This means that you can find a Jacob wool suitable to make almost any project you can dream of. Staple length is from 3 to 7 inches, which gives the fiber enough length to avoid pilling and make long-lasting fabrics. Crimp structure can vary within the same fleece in the differently colored portions.

A commercially processed Jacob wool is available in black, as well as other colors. This is usually a British Jacob, which can feel a little coarser than the American wool, but I suspect that a fleece handpicked from a British Jacob shepherd will feel a bit more next-to-skin worthy than the large-scale processed top from a wool pool. That said, however, mill-processed Jacob fiber is lovely to spin. The fibers glide past each other to make a beautiful yarn that's a pleasure to use for any project.

As of 2012, American Jacob is categorized on The Livestock Conservancy list as threatened, which means that there are fewer than one thousand new animals registered in one year and fewer than five thousand animals in the world.

Sampling Jacob

❶ 2-ply woolen-spun. For this sample, I opened and fluffed the locks thoroughly, so they were no longer recognizable. I then spun from this cloud of fiber using a woolen draft and plied to a 2-ply. The result is an extremely lumpy and inconsistent yarn, and the knitted sample is very rustic looking. Both are nice to handle, with plenty of springiness. It's not the yarn I was looking for, but it could make a beautiful everyday sweater or a fun woven fabric.

❷ 2-ply, somewhat worsted-spun. I did this sample a bit differently. Instead of working the locks completely open as I did with sample 1, I just took the locks, moved my forefinger and thumb over the cut end to open it slightly, and began to spin worsted-style from the cut end, giving a much more consistent yarn. It is all white, just because there were no black fibers in the handful of wool I picked up. This yarn is very flexible, with a bit more body, but it doesn't feel very soft. An exciting thing happened when I made it into the lace and woven swatches, however. It changed character somewhat: Both fabrics feel like something you could wear next to your skin. If the sett of the woven sample were a bit closer, it would be appropriate for a summer wool skirt; left as is, it could be a beautiful wrap. I finished the woven swatch with an aggressive washing, and it shrank only a little.

To prepare the fiber for this Jacob cardigan, I washed the fleece and separated it into white, black, and two shades of gray groups. I knit it circularly from the top down using Elizabeth Zimmermann's percentage system and then steeked it. Jacob is a wonderful fleece with which to experiment with color gradation.

1

— Jacob —
hand opened and
thoroughly fluffed/
woolen-spun from
the cloud/
2-ply

2

— Jacob —
hand opened/
cut end opened
slightly/
worsted-spun
from the cut end/
2-ply

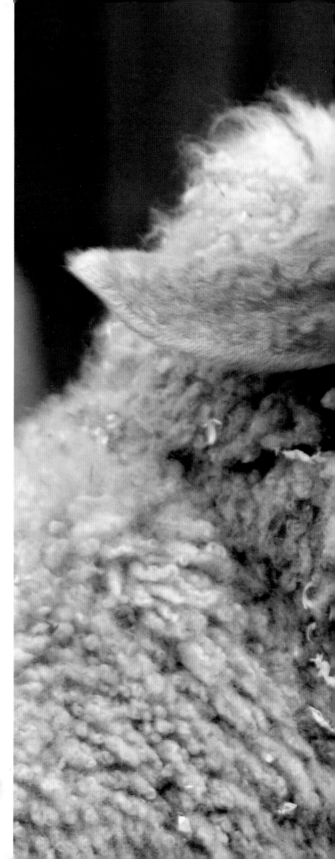

TUNIS

Also known as American Tunis, Tunis is a
fat-tailed sheep (see page 198). These sheep
are sometimes referred to as broad tail or
Barbary, so you may hear Tunis sheep referred
to as Tunisian Barbary. It is actually the oldest
sheep breed developed in America; its ancestors were imported in the late 1700s as a gift
to the United States from the ruler of Tunisia
and commended to Judge Richard Peters of
Pennsylvania. Judge Peters crossed these fat-
tailed imports with locally available sheep,
probably Southdown and English Leicester,
and then made rams available and gave away
lambs to spread the breed. In *A Report of the
Sheep Industry of the U.S.*, published in 1892, Ezra
Carmen wrote, "But for the introduction of
the fine-wooled Merino, these Tunisian sheep
would probably have become disseminated
throughout the U.S., and in some of them
have become the prevailing flocks." From
Pennsylvania, this breed spread along the East
Coast to New England; most Southern flocks
were wiped out during the Civil War. The
majority of today's flocks are on the East Coast.

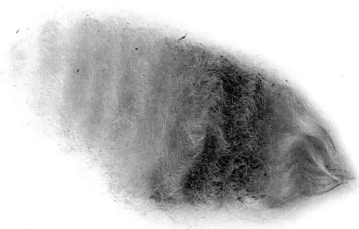

Tunis sheep are medium size and docile. They can thrive on marginal land, are disease resistant, and tolerate both heat and cold. Because the breed is so low maintenance, it is once again gaining popularity and spreading across the United States, although as of 2012, they are on The Livestock Conservancy's watch list, which means there are fewer than 2,500 registrations annually and fewer than 10,000 of the breed in the world.

Being a fat-tailed sheep, Tunis is like the Karakul discussed in chapter 7 (page 196). If I were categorizing sheep by background only, the Tunis would be in the same category as the Karakul, but I used wool characteristics to form the categorizations I made, and this wool does not resemble that of the strong, dual-coated Karakul. The reasons for including Tunis in this chapter are complicated, and I wavered back and forth before deciding. Wool categorization is not an absolute, however, and many wool types fit comfortably in more groups than one.

In their *In Sheep's Clothing,* Nola and Jane Fournier categorize Tunis as a Down-type wool, and I surely could agree. It is a very bouncy, springy wool, similar to others in the Down-type group. Its very fine crimp (about 8 to 10 crimps per inch) is not very consistent from the butt to the tip of the triangular lock, and it is sometimes disorganized in the lock. In addition to those Down-type characteristics, its fiber diameter could qualify it to be included with my group of fine-wool breeds. Fiber diameters range from 24 to 31 microns. As we've seen, wool from Merino sheep can be as thick as 26 microns and Corriedale up to 35 microns,

yet both of these are firmly in my finewools category because of their lock shape and crimp structure. Compared to these, therefore, the fleece of Tunis, which is generally thought of as a meat producer, can be happily worn next to the skin and, with its fine crimp and low fiber diameter, could easily be included with my fine wools.

The fleeces of Tunis sheep are generally 4 to 6 inches long, with a weight of 6 to 15 pounds. The fleece is light for its bulk, which means that you could knit a lightweight, warm sweater more easily with this wool than with some others with a lower volume-to-weight ratio. When I considered all of these characteristics, I decided that it just wasn't similar enough to either the fine wools or Down types for me, and so I placed it in the "Other" category, which means that I can prepare this wool any way I want to! (Of course, that, in fact, stands true for any wool.)

When the lambs are born, they are double coated, with an allover reddish-cinnamon color. As they mature, this reddish color remains on their head and legs, but the wool turns a creamy white, and the dual coat disappears. Some fleece may have some reddish or tan fibers in it that are slightly thicker in diameter than the white wool fibers, though the breed standard discourages any colored fibers. Also, though rare, there may be some kemp fibers found in the fleece. The fleece I spun for the Tunis samples had a bit of kemp in it, though not enough to make any difference in my end-result yarn. The kemp fibers were short and not very coarse, and most fell out while spinning.

— Tunis —
*hand opened/
woolen-spun/
2-ply*

— Tunis —
*hand opened cut
end/
woolen-spun/
3-ply*

Sampling Tunis

❶ Tunis spun from opened locks. I spun this sample after just opening the locks with my fingers and pulling the wool apart over and over until it formed a cloud. I had difficulty controlling this yarn, and it was very inconsistent.

❷ & ❸ 2- and 3-ply spun with no fiber prep. Next, I spun from a portion of the fleece without doing any prep. I found that this was the way to get the smoothest, most consistent yarn: just spin the fleece woolen without using any fiber-prep tools. Although these yarns are a bit inconsistent, too, some of this can be attributed to the fact that this particular fleece had a lot of second cuts and short fibers. As I spun the singles for these samples, I removed the second cuts before adding twist. This process can be a little time-consuming at first, but with practice, you learn to remove the second cuts with just a little pick and flick of your fingers while you continue to spin. Although some of the short bits do get by, this is nothing to really worry about unless you are planning to enter the skein in a competition. I made 2- and 3-ply yarns from my singles. As you can see from the samples, much of the inconsistency is camouflaged in the fabric swatches I knit and wove with the yarns.

The 3-ply yarn (2) is elastic and cushy, and the sample I knit with it is extremely stretchy. Even if knit at a firmer gauge, this is not a fabric I would make a skirt or dress out of, but it would be a great sweater. In addition, if I spun it more finely, I could see making a pair of hard-wearing socks with it. The fact that the lock was disturbed very little before spinning kept the fibers mostly aligned, which contributes to its resistance to pilling, whereas the woolen spinning allows plenty of bounce to remain in the yarn.

The fabric woven with the 2-ply yarn (3, facing page) also has a lovely amount of spring, because even before spinning, the Tunis fiber is bouncy and lush. Though it doesn't have the fineness of Cormo or Merino, I certainly would be willing to wear this particular sample next to my skin. You must make this decision on a fleece-by-fleece basis, however, because you'll find a wide range of fiber diameters in this breed.

❹ Tunis spun from handcarded rolags. For the yarns opposite, I spun singles from hand-carded rolags (see page 159), then made 2- and 3-ply yarns. I wove a swatch with the 2-ply yarn, and knit a swatch from the 3-ply yarn, so I could compare these swatches with those made of yarns spun from unprepped fleece. I found it more difficult to spin a consistent yarn from my rolags. The carding blended the second cuts and short bits in with the longer staples, making it much more difficult to remove any unwanted pieces as I spun.

Both of these samples are softer in feel, but they definitely have more of a tendency to pill than the unprocessed samples do. Even with the inconsistency apparent in all the woolen-spun samples in this chapter, it's yet another example that inconsistencies are often obscured in the final fabrics. All yarn that holds together is usable yarn.

3

— *Tunis* —
handcarded/
woolen-spun from
rolags/
2-ply

4

— *Tunis* —
handcarded/
woolen-spun from
rolags/
3-ply

❺ & ❻ Tunis spun from top pulled through a diz. To prepare the fleece for these yarns, I pulled combed fiber through a diz into top. I then spun the top using a worsted drafting method. These yarns are the smoothest and most consistent of my Tunis yarns. It was a bit easier to spin a fine yarn with fiber prepared this way, though I believe that the unprepped fiber would have behaved just as well if I had coaxed it finer as I spun the singles.

I wove the 2-ply sample (5), and also used it to knit a lace swatch. This was the only one of the Tunis yarns that I used to knit lace because, although its inconsistencies don't show in solid weaving or knitting, the openwork of lace makes lumps and bumps more apparent. This smooth yarn doesn't have the luster of a longwool, but light seems to bounce off it, and while the lace doesn't have the drape of a piece knit with heavier wool, it does look warm and inviting.

The stockinette swatch I made with the 3-ply yarn (6) from combed top is gorgeous. Its resilience is similar to that of the other samples, but it has a more finished feel compared to them, especially the carded samples, which feel more rustic.

Because I prepped and spun the yarns for these swatches worsted-style, the fabrics will be more likely to resist wear. Though pills may turn up with frequent abrasion, garments made with these yarns would be the ones you throw on every day for years with very little maintenance.

5

— *Tunis* —
combed and dizzed/
worsted-spun/
2-ply

6

— *Tunis* —
combed and dizzed/
worsted-spun/
3-ply

GLOSSARY OF TERMS

BATT. A sheet of carded fibers.

BRADFORD COUNT. A measurement of how many 560-yard skeins of singles yarn can theoretically be spun from 1 pound of top.

BUMP. A cylinder of coiled fibers prepared for spinning, weighing about 22 pounds (10 kilos).

BUTT. The cut end of a lock of wool.

CARD. *See* Handcard

CARDING CLOTH. A leather or rubber mat with metal pins; used on handcards and drum carders. Pins are set at different distances apart, depending on the type of fiber to be carded.

CLOUD. Fibers that have been opened up but not carded, combed, or organized further. Most times a cloud consists of shorter-stapled fibers. This preparation is simply spun by handfuls.

COMBING MILK. A preparation applied to fleece before combing or carding it. It is designed to cut down on static and control fibers. Also called spinning oil.

COMBS. Tools with from 1 to 5 rows of very long tines used for removing short fibers and aligning wool for worsted spinning. Also known as wool combs, handcombs.

CRIMP, CRIMP STRUCTURE. Regular wave over the length of wool fibers (also naturally occurring in some other protein fibers). Crimp can also be created in manmade fibers to introduce some of the effects of naturally occurring crimp.

DEMI-LUSTER. A soft glow or partial luster.

DIZ. A concave tool with one or several small holes to pull fiber through to make long strips of combed top or roving.

DRAFT. The act of drawing out an amount of fibers from the fiber supply before adding twist to make yarn.

DRUMCARDER. A tool with two or more drums covered with carding cloth; used for opening fibers and aligning them in preparation for spinning.

DUAL-COATED. *See* Multicoat

EVEN WEAVE. A fabric in which the number of picks per inch (horizontal threads) matches the number of ends per inch (vertical threads) in woven cloth.

FELT. The compaction of wool fibers using heat, water, friction, and soap to form the wool into a solid mass. Usually done with unspun fibers. Irreversible.

FIBER CIGAR. A carded preparation in which the fleece is removed from the card as a small batt, then, starting at one side edge, rolled so that the fibers are lengthwise and parallel on the "cigar."

FINISHING. Sometimes referred to as setting. Allowing the fibers to relax into each other after spinning by submerging them in water and allowing them to dry; sometimes combined with plunging or smacking the yarn against a hard surface, depending on the result being sought.

FLICK CARD, FLICKER. A tool designed to open the fibers in each lock of wool.

FULL OR FULLING. Uses a process similar to felting (friction, water, soap), except that the fibers have been spun into yarn. Fulling can be done to strengthen yarn or as a finishing process for fabric.

GREASE. Grease in wool is a combination of pure lanolin, sweat, dirt, and other impurities.

HALO. Ends of fibers that work free from the spun yarn and create a soft fluff around the outside of the yarn and/or finished object.

HAND. How the yarn or fabric feels.

HANDCARD. A tool covered in carding cloth for opening fibers and aligning them in preparation for spinning; usually used in pairs.

IN THE GREASE. Unwashed fleece, right off the sheep.

KEMP. A wiry fiber, much like crimpy hair in appearance; usually quite thick.

LANOLIN. A wax secreted by the sheep that coats the outside of the fibers.

LICKER-IN. The smaller drum of a drumcarder that pulls the fibers into the carder and deposits fibers on the main drum. It spins in the opposite direction of the main drum, and this opposite movement helps to open and separate the fibers.

LINEN TESTER. A small magnifier that has a scale built in. It is usually used in finished fabrics to count the number of warp and weft threads but can be used for counting twists per inch or crimps per inch in spun yarn.

LOCK, LOCK SHAPE. A small cluster of fibers that tend to stick together when the sheep is shorn. A lock is usually about finger or thumb sized, and, depending on the sheep's breed, varies in shape, from square and blocky to long and pointy.

LONG DRAW. A drafting method in which the twist is allowed to enter the fiber supply, which results in a yarn with good insulating properties.

MEASURING MAGNIFIER. *See* Linen tester

MICRON MEASUREMENT. The expressed measurement is an average of the diameters of the fibers in the sample, measured in microns. Measurement often used to be done with a microscope but is now done with a laser.

MULTICOAT. A fleece that contains fibers of different textures and lengths. Refers to either the undercoat, which provides warmth to the animal and is generally soft and usually shorter than the outercoat, or to the outercoat or guard hairs, which are generally more coarse than the undercoat.

NEPS. Imperfections caused by fibers that are immature or haven't been straightened properly.

NOIL. Waste and knots of wool that may happen during processing.

ORIFICE. The opening at the front of the spinning wheel flyer through which the yarn must travel before being wound onto the bobbin. Some spinning wheels have open orifices (not a hole), making them easy to thread.

ORIFICE HOOK. The hook for threading yarn or a leader through the flyer orifice before spinning.

OVERDYE. Cover an existing color (not white) with a new color.

PLAIN WEAVE. A fabric in which each warp thread and weft thread intersects with each other in a simple over/under pattern.

PRIMITIVE BREED. Older breeds of sheep that have not been "improved" by crossing with other breeds. Their lineage can be traced back hundreds of years or sometimes more.

PSI. Pins per square inch, a measurement denoting the spacing of pins in carding cloth; sometimes expressed as tpi (teeth per inch). *See also* tpi

PURL. An S-shaped crimp characteristic of breeds with long, curly locks, such as Wensleydale. It is called purl because it resembles the look of yarn that has been knit and then unravelled.

RAW FLEECE. Fleece or wool that is right off the sheep, prior to any cleaning or processing.

ROLAG. A fiber preparation, usually for woolen spinning, that has been handcarded and then rolled up into a tube.

ROVING. A long strand of carded fibers, generally made on large carding drums in a mill and then drawn off the drums into narrow strips; it can also be made by the spinner, using a drumcarder.

SCOUR. Remove lanolin and dirt from fleece.

SCURF. Skin flakes (like dandruff).

SECOND CUTS. Short bits of fleece that result when the shearer runs the clippers down the sheep a second time, re-shearing a spot.

SETT. In weaving, the number of warp threads in a given measure of the fabric width.

SHORT FORWARD DRAW. *See* Worsted spun

SINGLES. Yarn that has been spun in one direction but has not been plied.

SKIRTING. The process of removing dung tags and stained areas around the outside of the fleece, as well as belly and neck wool.

SORTING WOOL. Many breeds of sheep have wool that can vary in length and crimp over the whole fleece. Sorting separates these different wool lengths and textures based on the part of the sheep they come from, for example, neck, back, leg, shoulders, sides, and so on.

SPINNING OIL. *See* Combing milk

STAPLE. The length of the lock when it is not extended or stretched.

TEASING TOOL. A device covered with carding cloth and used to open locks before feeding them through a drumcarder.

TOP. A long, even length of fibers that have been combed; generally used for worsted spinning.

TPI. Twists per inch in the spun yarn. Tpi may also refer to "teeth per inch" in carding cloth. *See also* psi.

TWIST. The magical structural element that holds the fibers together and makes yarn. Different amounts of twist can change the way yarn acts. Less twist makes a soft, drapey yarn; more twist makes a durable yarn with body. Too little twist allows the fibers to drift apart; too much makes a yarn that feels harsh and brittle regardless of the fiber used.

VM. Vegetable matter, such as grain, grass, weeds, and so on, that got into the animal's fleece in the field.

WHORL. The small round part that the drive band goes around and is turned by the spinning of the drive wheel. Whorls can come in different sizes, affecting how much twist is added to the yarn being spun. Sometimes called a pulley.

WOOLEN-SPUN. Spun from carded fibers that are generally short, using long draw to draft the fibers out, allowing the twist to enter the fiber supply. The combination of the carded preparation and the long draw draft results in an airy and light yarn that is great for warmth and that is quickly spun.

WORSTED-SPUN. Spun from fibers that have been combed, drawn through a diz, and then spun with a short forward draw with no twist entering the fiber supply. This combination of aligned fibers and short forward draw results in a yarn that is dense and compact, and therefore good for durable items; it is also yarn with a crisp look, ideal for color separations and cable designs.

WRAPS PER INCH (WPI). A way of measuring the thickness of yarn. Much like gauge in knitting, the wpi measurement can vary from person to person but can be a good way to compare handspun yarns. It is done by loosely wrapping yarn in a 1-inch width so that the strands touch but are not bunched up. The yarn should also not be stretched tightly. The number of strands that can fit in the 1-inch width is the wpi measurement.

METRIC CONVERSIONS

to get	to get	to get
centimeters	meters	meters
when you know	when you know	when you know
inches	feet	yards
multiply by	multiply by	multiply by
2.54	0.305	0.9144

FREQUENTLY USED MEASUREMENTS

INCHES	CENTIMETERS	INCHES	CENTIMETERS	INCHES	CENTIMETERS
0.5	1.27	8.5	21.59	23	58.42
1	2.54	9	22.86	24	60.96
1.5	3.81	9.5	24.13	25	63.50
2	5.08	10	25.40	26	66.04
2.5	6.35	11	27.94	27	68.58
3	7.62	12	30.48	28	71.12
3.5	8.89	13	33.02	29	73.66
4	10.16	14	35.56	30	76.20
4.5	11.43	15	38.10	31	78.74
5	12.70	16	40.64	32	81.28
5.5	13.97	17	43.18	33	83.82
6	15.24	18	45.72	34	86.36
6.5	16.51	19	48.26	35	88.90
7	17.78	20	50.80	36	91.44
7.5	19.05	21	53.34		
8	20.32	22	55.88		

USDA STANDARD
WOOL SPECIFICATIONS

TYPE OF WOOL	OLD BLOOD GRADE	NUMERICAL COUNT GRADE	LIMITS FOR AVERAGE FIBER DIAMETER (MICRONS)	VARIABILITY LIMIT FOR STANDARD DEVIATION MAXIMUM (MICRONS)
Fine	Fine	Finer than 80's	<17.70	3.59
Fine	Fine	80's	17.70–19.14	4.09
Fine	Fine	70's	19.15–20.59	4.59
Fine	Fine	64's	20.60–22.04	5.19
Medium	1/2 Blood	62's	22.05–23.49	5.89
Medium	1/2 Blood	60's	23.50–24.94	6.49
Medium	3/8 Blood	58's	24.95–26.39	7.09
Medium	3/8 Blood	56's	26.40–27.84	7.59
Medium	1/4 Blood	54's	27.85–29.29	8.19
Medium	1/4 Blood	50's	29.30–30.99	8.69
Coarse	Low 1/4	48's	31.00–32.69	9.09
Coarse	Low 1/4	46's	32.70–34.39	9.59
Coarse	Common	44's	34.40–36.19	10.09
Very coarse	Braid	40's	36.20–38.09	10.69
Very coarse	Braid	36's	38.10–40.20	11.19
Very coarse	Braid	Coarser than 36's	>40.20	—

The blood system for most all useful purposes is outdated and has not been recognized by USDA since 1955. From Colorado State University (www.ext.colostate.edu/pubs/livestk/01401.html)

READING LIST

Amos, Alden. *The Alden Amos Big Book of Handspinning*. Interweave, 2001.

Anderson, Enid. *The Spinner's Encyclopedia*. Sterling, 1987.

Anderson, Sarah. *The Spinner's Book of Yarn Designs: Techniques for Creating 80 Yarns*. Storey Publishing, 2012.

British Wool Marketing Board. *British Sheep & Wool: A Guide to British Sheep Breeds and Their Unique Wool*. British Wool Marketing Board, 2010.

Fannin, Allen. *Handspinning: Art and Technique*. Van Nostrand Reinhold, 1970.

Field, Anne. *Spinning Wool: Beyond the Basics*, rev. ed. Trafalgar Square, 2010.

Fournier, Nola and Jane Fournier. *In Sheep's Clothing: A Handspinner's Guide to Wool*. Interweave, 1995.

Franquemont, Abby. *Respect the Spindle*. Interweave, 2009.

King, Amy. *Spin Control: Techniques for Spinning the Yarn You Want*. Interweave, 2009.

Lamb, Sara. *Spin to Weave: The Weaver's Guide to Making Yarn*. Interweave, 2013.

McCuin, Judith MacKenzie. *The Intentional Spinner*. Interweave, 2009.

Parkes, Clara. *The Knitter's Book of Socks*. Potter Craft, 2011.

———. *The Knitter's Book of Wool: The Ultimate Guide to Understanding, Using, and Loving This Most Fabulous Fiber*. Potter Craft, 2009.

Robson, Deborah, and Carol Ekarius. *The Fleece & Fiber Sourcebook: More Than 200 Fibers, from Animal to Spun Yarn*. Storey Publishing, 2011.

———. *The Field Guide to Fleece: 100 Sheep Breeds and How to Use Their Fibers*. Storey Publishing, 2013.

Ross, Mabel. *The Encyclopedia of Handspinning*. Interweave, 1988.

———. *The Essentials of Handspinning,* rev. ed. Crook of Devon, 1984.

———. *The Essentials of Yarn Design for Handspinners*. Crook of Devon, 1986.

Ryder, M. L. *Sheep & Man*. Duckworth, 2007.

Ryder, M. L., and S. K. Stephenson. *Wool Growth*. Academic Press, 1968.

Teal, Peter. *Hand Woolcombing and Spinning: A Guide to Worsteds from the Spinning Wheel*. Poole, 1976.

RESOURCES

BREED INFORMATION

American Sheep Industry Association
www.sheepusa.org

Breeds of Livestock
Oklahoma State University
www.ansi.okstate.edu/breeds

Grades and Lengths of Grease Wool
Colorado State University
www.ext.colostate.edu/pubs/livestk/01401.html
Micron counts

The Livestock Conservancy
www.livestockconservancy.org

Rare Breeds Survival Trust
www.rbst.org.uk

U.S. Sheep Breeders Online Directory
www.nebraskasheep.com

OTHER RESOURCES

craigslist
www.craigslist.com
Use craigslist to find used tools and equipment in your local area that you can go and see in person.

Hokett Would Work
http://wouldworkifhewantedto.wordpress.com
Hokett loom

Ravelry
www.ravelry.com
Ravelry has several groups dedicated only to helping spinners find used tools they may be interested in. In addition, most manufacturers have their own groups with threads dedicated to selling and buying used items.

Spinners', Weavers' & Knitters' Housecleaning Pages
www.kbbspin.org
A free place to find and sell wool stuff

Unicorn Fibre
www.unicornfibre.com
Unicorn Power Scour

ACKNOWLEDGMENTS

I'm not sure where to begin with all of the thank-yous that I owe, so I'll just start with my family: My never-ending love and gratitude go to my charming husband, Lou, and the kids who've lived with me throughout this process — Chelsea, Maggie, and Ryan. I was at times unbearable, I've forgotten how to cook, and I haven't helped to clean the house in years; but on the bright side, there has always been a comfortable pile of wool to lounge on. Thank you for your patience. And thank you to my eldest, Brittney DeFriez, who listened to me cry and complain on the phone and sometimes I even forgot to ask how she was doing.

I could not have done this book at all without the help of my much-loved friend Jillian Moreno, who listened, discussed, pushed, encouraged, rescheduled, nudged, and sometimes scolded me. She knew what I needed and came through every time.

Jacey Boggs, Amy King, and Sara Lamb were fabulous when I called to argue about the technical points of spinning. We may not always agree, but just having the chance to hash things out with them is an enormous opportunity, and I don't take their friendship for granted.

Deborah Robson has been an inspiration and a mentor for many years now. She is kind and sharing and has been encouraging to me ever since this project was just a seed of an idea.

The people at Storey Publishing have been wonderful to work with and have been patient with my many questions and my worries and endless emails. I am so thankful to my editor Gwen Steege and her calm voice that I could recognize even in her written messages to me. I would also like to thank Alethea Morrison for her wonderful design, which made this book a beautiful thing. Also, John Polak, the photographer, who was somehow able to get photos of things I thought would be impossible.

Thank you to my fearless parents, Cookie and Malcolm Shearer. My dad always made me feel like the favorite child and still does, which was a great boost to my self-esteem. My mom always made me believe that I could do whatever I set out to do. She did this by her great example of hard work and always being willing to try new things. I love them and admire them both.

I appreciate all of the shepherds whom I have worked with, both for supplying fleeces for the Spinning Loft as well as for this book. They love their sheep, and they have been so helpful to me. One in particular is Neil Kentner. I've known Neil for years, and he is one of the best fleece judges I've ever met, and he always calls me to come and see his new lambs.

Over the years I have had a lot of teachers. Many of them I have met in person and some I just know from their published work. I am thankful to them for their willingness to share their knowledge and their dedication to spinning and to asking the deepest questions. I hope that this book is a tribute to them and the things I have learned. I would like to express my thanks to Betty Forsythe, my first spinning teacher. In particular, and in addition to those wonderful women already mentioned, I would like to express my thanks to Maggie Casey, Anne Field, Abby Franquemont, Stephenie Gaustad, Clara Parkes, Jane Patrick, Mabel Ross, Margaret Stove, and Peter Teal. I know there are so many more.

The people at *SpinOff* magazine also provided a great boost to my self confidence. As I first dipped my toes into writing about spinning, they believed in my abilities and helped me trust myself.

And finally, to all of those who have spun with me for fun and in classes, those who encouraged me and those who began as customers in my little spinning shop and became good friends over the years, I would like to say thank you. I feel honored that you believe in me.

INDEX

MORE BOOKS TO KEEP YOU SPINNING!

448 pages. Hardcover with jacket.
ISBN 978-1-60342-711-1.

232 pages. Paper.
ISBN 978-1-61212-178-9.

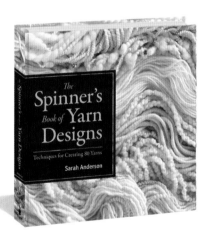

256 pages. Hardcover with 32 technique
cards in an envelope.
ISBN 978-1-60342-738-8.

168 pages. Hardcover with
concealed wire-o.
ISBN 978-1-60342-468-4.

These and other books from Storey Publishing are available
wherever quality books are sold or by calling 1-800-441-5700.
Visit us at www.storey.com or sign up for our newsletter
at www.storey.com/signup.